the battle between *good* and *evil*

By: Patricia Kelley

This book is dedicated to *God* and the *Collective*. I am truly grateful for the gifts/abilities that *God* bestowed upon me before birth. I am grateful to have been able to keep that door open throughout my life so as to be able to share my gifts/abilities with others for the purpose of helping. And I am grateful for the *Collective* who have helped me in so many ways on my journey thus far while on this Earthly plane.

Table of Contents

Introduction

Battle, always a battle. From the beginning of time there has been some kind of battle. We battle every day over one thing or another. We battle over food, places to sleep, places to live, making purchases, getting good deals, driving, conversation, opinions, countries, the color of skin, ethnicities, relationships, opinions. It is practically endless if you think about it. And yes, they are battles. We battle for freedom to live a certain way, in a certain place. We battle over freedom of speech, over freedom for this and that. It never seems to end. But the scariest battle of all is the battle between "good" and "evil" in the religious and Spiritual world that spills over into the lives of every Human on this planet and every life form on Earth, on other Planets, in other Galaxies, and Dimensions.

There is a battle between Religion, Atheism, Spiritualism, Metaphysics, and any other sects or categories that Humans put themselves into. When born, a Human is either born into a Religious family, a Spiritual family, a Metaphysical family, an Atheist family, or any other sect or category the parents and/or family believes in and practice. As the Human grows and enters the world outside of the family, the Human becomes exposed to a great deal of information, education, opinions, and more. They either then stick with their born sect or at some point decide for themselves if they want to join another religion, seek Spiritualism, Metaphysics, or drop their born family religion and become an Atheist because they either have decided they do not believe that particular religion, or they feel they do not fit into any other or even believe there is

God. They can also feel confused and therefore practice no religion at all. And they can also not define themselves as an Atheist either. There is a battle that happens within them. Being born into a highly religious family and deciding at some point in life you do not believe or want to be part of that religion can cause great conflict within the family and/or the Human themselves. The battle outside and inside becomes "good" versus "evil" which is caused most of the time by guilt.

This is the battle that should scare the heck out of you because it is real. It affects everything inside of a Human and other life forms, and outside of them as well. It affects the Humans and other life forms they love. It affects how they live their lives and where they live their lives. It affects their actions and inactions. It affects their speech and nonspeech. It affects their emotional, mental, and physical health. It affects their decisions they make for themselves and for the others that they love and/or care for. It affects their thoughts and the words they speak and don't speak.

For Humans, even competition in life as in playing card games, board games, video games, gambling, all sports and more there is "good" and "evil." The "good" plays or competes and wins fairly, while the "evil" plays or competes looking for a way to cheat or actually cheats.

"Good" and "evil" resides in all Humans and other life forms whether born with it, affected by it, or inflicted with it while living their lives on the Earthly plane.

All Humans were birthed with love and good. They were created with and for love. Unfortunately, with the Dark Energies/Entities, a Human or other life form can be born with "good" but can also be born with "evil" due to possible possession by a Dark Energy/Entity. That may not be known immediately, but in time and with growth of the Human or other life form, it will be revealed in some way.

Battle between "good" and "evil" can rage inside a Human or other life form their entire lives if corrupted by the Devil, a Demon, or Dark Energy/Entity. It can completely overshadow the "good" the Human or other life form was born with. The darkness can take over completely almost erasing the "good" in the Human or other life form. But for some, a rage inside between "good" and "evil" can take place due to the "good" battling the "evil" trying to restore the "good" back into the Human or other life form. And the Human or other life form can be tormented and tortured by this experience that is taking place within them. They may not even know or understand completely what is happening to them, yet they know that their thoughts and actions reflect something to the effect of "good" and "evil."

The battle between "good" and "evil" on Earth, on other Planets, and in other Galaxies, and Dimensions will never end. It may look or feel like it is ending or might end, but it never will as long as there is life on Earth, on other Planets, in other Galaxies, and Dimensions.

the battle between *good* and *evil*

Chapter 1

Questions for God

The battle between "good" and "evil" prompts Humans to ask questions of God. They start to wonder why God even created Humans. They wonder why they are here on Earth. They want to know what their purpose is on Earth. They want to know why animals are here because "evil" exists towards them as well as Humans. They want to know if God really exists since there is so much darkness that roams the Earth. And they want to know what exactly is **the battle between "good" and "evil?"**

Since God is the only one who can give those answers to Humans, I decided to ask God on behalf of all Humans that would like to have answers to those questions. It went like this. I asked the questions and God spoke the answers.

God, why are we here?

You are here because I, God, created you. I created every living being on Earth, on other Planets, in other Galaxies, and Dimensions. Let's start with the beginning of Humans.

In order to survive on Earth, I had to design such a being that would be able to live in this atmosphere and to be able to sustain themselves and this planet, your planet. Different forms and appearances were needed for procreation. I

1

designed the basics and with what Earth offered; the Human race evolved. Some evolved from other forms on Earth such as from animal life forms, amphibious life forms, reptile life forms, and insect life forms. Those grew to Human forms eons ago.

I gave Earth life in all forms, and they evolved in all different forms and ways, and all able to procreate in some way. There were life forms that did not survive, and some died off and were killed off by Humans when Humans evolved to more upright and somewhat intelligent beings.

What the Humans evolved from and the way they evolved played a part in the way they look different from one another. The different parts of Earth and its environment played a part in the Human physical appearance as did the climate and way of life to be able to live and survive. Humans have been around a very long time in some form or another. Humans at a certain point were able to procreate, thus "Man" and "Woman." Humans developed from the sea, and from life inside and outside of the planet Earth.

The purpose of Humans was to procreate and populate Earth with the Human species. They were to grow Earth and take care of it. All Humans were necessary for Earth because other life forms were not able to grow and sustain Earth as I intended it to. So, Humans had to form and grow into beings with a higher intelligence than other species on Earth in order to be able to do this.

Other life forms were also needed for Earth to procreate in their way. Each living being from plant life, to animal life, to insect life, and more were given a purpose for Earth. And each living being including Humans have Souls. Souls are the life force of the physical bodies. Without a Soul there is no life.

I did not create life forms on Earth to have their lives taken on purpose because each life form has a particular purpose in order to sustain Earth. There is no life form on Earth that has no purpose. And that applies to life in the ocean, in other bodies of water, on the land, and in the air.

If a life form or species is killed to extinction the Humans and Earth suffer even if Humans do not see it that way. Earth and Humans suffer because as I said, all living beings have a purpose on and for Earth just as Humans have their purpose for being here. If a species is killed to extinction, then there will not be that life form or species again on Earth. The only possible way an extinct species would be brought back to Earth would be if DNA of that extinct species was found and Humans find a way to possibly bring it back to life. That DNA would be rare to find if found at all.

As a Human being, you do not exist on any other Planets, in any other Galaxies, or Dimensions. You were created for Earth and Earth alone.

What is my purpose?

The purpose of Humans was meant to procreate and populate the Earth. They were meant to grow the Earth in all ways. Humans were meant to evolve to points in order to sustain Earth and grow it stronger and more beautiful.

The minds of Humans were to grow and expand and become more educated in order to and learn how to take care of Earth as they were to take care of each other. Humans were designed

3

to love and help each other and the other life forms on Earth, and to live in unison and harmony.

Each Human was designed uniquely and with each birth still be unique. Each Human has a purpose on Earth as does all other life forms. No two Humans are the same, not even twins, triplets, etc. There is still somewhat of a difference in those. And the same goes for insects, animals, ocean life, etc.

The question of what is my purpose developed when Humans evolved to a more intelligent species. It came when groups were formed in some way as in Spiritual groups, religions of various forms, and even those who had no belief in a religion or Spirituality.

Humans were created on Earth to grow and evolve. They were meant to procreate and have families to leave on Earth to continue growing and caring for Earth when their bodies died. They were meant to spread love, joy, and peace throughout Earth to other Human Beings and other life forms.

Humans were meant to help each other in all ways. They were meant to help other life forms grow and prosper and keep those species growing on Earth. Humans were meant to take care of Earth's beautiful trees, plants, flowers, and all foliage keeping them alive and thriving because plant life was meant as sustenance for Humans to consume and survive. That foliage was also meant to clean the air and keep it clean. Humans were meant to keep the ocean and beautiful bodies of water clean and free from contaminants.

Forests were meant for Humans to use trees to build shelter but not to deplete the forests. When trees were cut, then more were to be planted to take their place so that there would not be an ending supply. Forests were and are needed for other life forms to grow and survive and for Humans as well. They were and are desperately important and needed for the Earth.

Humans want to know individually what their purpose is here on Earth. Although Humans have evolved from different life forms and areas, each Human is different from the other, and so is their purpose here on the Earthly plane. God gave Humans free will to make choices and decisions for themselves. They were given the choice to do what they want and to be what they want while here on Earth. Those decisions and choices represent the part the Human plays here.

Some make contributions in their lives by inventing things for the good and possible growth of Humans. Other Humans make decisions to enter a certain field of work that allows them to make contributions in that arena. Some Humans spend their lives helping plant life grow and survive which might also include wildlife in all forms. Other Humans enter the healing field, and so on.

It's what a Human feels inside of themselves about their own life. Not every Human has to make a marked contribution on the planet. Just by a Human being here on Earth is purpose because they would not be here if they didn't have a purpose. But Humans have developed the mindset that they have to do something big or specific to matter or feel like they belong here. Living a good and loving life on Earth is purpose enough. Being a good Human to yourself and to others is purpose enough. Staying off a negative path is purpose enough. Helping other Humans in positive ways is purpose enough. Being kind to animals and other life forms is purpose enough.

Humans were taught by many other Humans that they have to contribute something significant in order to have purpose. That just isn't so.

When Humans get on a wrong path, one that can be a detriment to themselves and/or to others, but gets themselves back on the right path, that is purpose enough. If they take their experiences from negative to positive and share with others, that's purpose enough for their life.

Humans working in service professions in all capacities is purpose enough to be here on Earth. Humans who birth other Humans for good cause is purpose enough. I can go on and on. Humans need to know that their life here on the Earthly plane has purpose in and of itself.

Even when Humans end up corrupted by the Devil, Demons, or Dark Energies/Entities, they have a purpose. Humans learn from other Humans. They also learn from the other life forms on Earth. There is purpose in every Human and every life form here. No Human or life form would be on Earth if they didn't have purpose.

Humans show their purpose in so many ways but don't even realize it because their name isn't up in lights so to speak, or become some famous or wealthy Humans. Humans, no matter what capacity in life they are in, have a purpose. It's all in the mind and the Human's perspective of themselves. It is also not allowing other Humans to make them feel as if they are less than them for any reason. Even if a Human never worked a day in their life while on the Earthly plane, they still have a purpose for being here. There will be something they say or do that will be a contribution in some way whether big or small and they may not even realize it.

Some Humans are obsessed with needing to find out exactly what their purpose is for being on Earth. They feel unfulfilled not knowing exactly what that is instead of just knowing that their presence here on Earth living their life is enough. It is the purpose, and that their presence is serving a purpose. They will see that in all things they do throughout their life. They just need to open their eyes, change their mindset and perspective and realize that. It would bring such comfort and joy to those Humans.

Does God exist?

Is God a person or a thing? God is everything and God is nothing. God is everywhere at the same time. God is love and peace. There is God whom all life forms know.

When Humans evolved to a certain degree of intelligence the question of God's existence came to minds. Most Humans began questioning God's existence when grief struck them, or bad or terrible things happened to them and others on Earth. The question was if God exists then why didn't he stop the terrible things from happening not understanding that God gave Humans free will, and that the Devil, Demons, and Dark Energies/Entities roam the Earth spreading their disease of hate, sickness, possession, death, and more all around.

Free will was given to Humans from the beginning of their existence in the form that they started on this planet. Then their intelligence grew with their brain evolvement and development. This intelligence was used to do good or bad. Humans always have had choices. Humans were not created to do bad things to themselves and/or to other life forms. Their free will and intelligence were directed to their choices.

The Devil, Demons, and Dark Energies/Entities tempted Humans from the beginning. When the Humans had free will with a lower intelligence before the intelligence developed to a higher degree, the temptations may not have appeared as bad things. But when the brain developed and intelligence grew, that and free will became factors in their choices. And also, to differentiate between bad and good and not allow themselves to be tempted into doing bad things or making bad decisions and mistakes.

However, in the Human's defense, the Devil, Demons, and Dark Energies/Entities were and are clever in using disguises in all forms to corrupt the Humans. If the Humans took the corrupted path, they at that point, had the choice, free will again, to get back on the right path in life. However, if they were possessed by Dark Energies/Entities it may have, and still could present a different outcome because the Human would no longer be in charge of their actions to make a positive decision or get back on a right path.

God is in the heart and Soul of every living being from low intelligence to the highest intelligence. God has allowed Humans to use their free will throughout their entire lives on Earth. God has stepped aside to allow Humans to make their own choices in life and to deal with and live with those choices. The only time God will intervene is if a Human's time is not up on the Earthly plane. God will then not allow that Human to die before their time.

Other Humans that pass on without God's intervention were meant to have their lives end at that point whether at the hands of other Humans, non-Humans, by their own hand, an accident, or even before, at birth, or shortly thereafter. Their Souls were needed elsewhere. In addition, their Souls may have come to the Earthly plane for a particular reason and

8

when that reason was fulfilled, then their physical body died sending the Soul back into the Universe. Others may have only wanted to experience Human life in certain capacities for as long as they needed to or wanted to. And God may have dispatched Souls to Earth to help others for a short time or longer.

These are some of the reasons God did not and does not intervene in what is deemed as a negative or tragic situation for a Human's life ending. Humans who loved the ones that have passed tragically or by accident will know at the end of their lives the reason for their loved one's passing when they did.

So, with this said, some Humans feel that God has abandoned them, does not love them, or even exist. They may feel that God hates them or their family and/or friends. So far from the truth. God allows Humans to live their lives. It's just like Human parents who need to allow their child/children to grow and experience life on their own and in their own way hopefully safely, and to make mistakes so that they can learn from them. It isn't easy for loving Human parents to do that but it is necessary for the child/children to survive here on Earth as adults while their parents are still alive here and when their parents' bodies die. It isn't easy for God either but he has to allow certain things to happen, but it doesn't mean he doesn't love his Human children.

God exists in everything Human and non-Human.

Groups at one point decided to worship what they knew or felt was God. From there other groups formed and more groups from there formed which is known as Religion. All these different groups or sects of Religion believed in one God. Some of those Religious groups believed in what they thought

9

God was to them. Other groups that formed calling themselves a Religion of some sort believed in actual material idols or statues calling those God and praying to them. Yet others believed that there was more than one God and worshiped different statues and non-statues praying to those. They prayed to different entities they felt were God.

Some groups didn't and don't believe there is God. They pray to no one and no thing. Most of those groups based their feelings on their experiences and non-experiences with God. If God didn't give them what they asked for then God didn't exist and doesn't exist. If God didn't do what they wanted then God didn't exist and doesn't exist. If a loved one's physical body was dying and God didn't heal them then God didn't exist and doesn't exist. If they didn't hear actual words from God then God didn't exist and doesn't exist. If God didn't stop battles and/or wars then God didn't exist and doesn't exist. The list goes on.

Then we have the dark groups that formed. Those dark groups didn't and don't believe in God nor did they ever or want to. Those groups worshipped and believed in the Devil, Demons, and Dark Energies/Entities. They worshipped and prayed to statues that represented dark and negative energies and to the Devil himself.

Those groups of people have been infected by the darkness and evil. Their brains have been corrupted in some way and swayed over to the dark side. Some of those Humans had been and are possessed by the Dark Energies/Entities. Some are controlled by the Devil and Demons. Their Souls have been infected and corrupted.

The Devil loves to recruit for the dark and to do evil and spread that infection throughout the Earth. The Devil will lie to

Humans making them believe there is no God and give them examples as proof. There is nothing the Devil won't do to corrupt Humans and bring them to the dark side to do his bidding in spreading evil.

The Devil will send Demons to try to sway God loving Humans to the dark side in tempting them in all ways be it with material goods, fame, money, status, and so much more.

The weak-willed Humans fall prey to this more than you can imagine. The down and out Humans having a very difficult time trying to survive fall prey to this. The greedy and money hungry fall prey to this. The mentally unstable fall prey to this. And it goes on and on. Not all Humans in these categories will be tempted and take the bait, but many have and will. And they are basically handing over their Soul to the darkness.

The mentally challenged and ill are major targets for the Devil and darkness. Many of the mentally ill have already been possessed by a Dark Energy/Entity. Other mentally ill have had accidents causing their illness. Others were born with a mental illness due to poor development of the brain or other issues, etc. and those are also targets for the Devil. However, those Humans who have mental illness from an accident or from birth, for example, guess who is really behind that. Who do you think caused the accident? And who do you think caused the poor development of the brain in birth? That's right, the darkness, evil.

The Devil will recruit whomever, wherever, and whenever for the dark side. And the Devil loves a challenge which is to bring a God loving Human who is healthy physically and mentally over to the dark side. Not easy to do, but in moments of weakness mentally, emotionally, or physically, the Devil has been successful.

Why are there Animals on Earth, and what is their purpose?

Animals were necessary for sustaining Earth as Humans and other life forms were. Many animals were for giving unconditional love to each other and Humans. Other animals were for keeping an overgrowing animal population down. Some animals were for keeping plant life in check. And others were to help Humans cultivate Earth as in helping plow fields to plant and grow food. These are just a few examples of the necessity of animals for Earth.

There is a reason and purpose for every living being on this planet. There is no animal or other life form that does not serve a purpose here on Earth.

From nothing to once a lush and peaceful Earth. Ocean, sea life, plant life, insect life, birds, etc. Earth at one point was a thing of peace and beauty. As life evolved and grew, Earth changed. Some for the good and some not so good. When Humans formed is when the problems started, but not initially and certainly not the intent of Humans for Earth.

Animals just as Humans can become infected with the darkness. If you think the Devil attacks only Humans, think again. There is nothing on this planet that the Devil won't attack or tempt to do or become evil.

The Devil has been around long before you think. Demons and Dark Energies/Entities as well. There isn't a Planet, Galaxy, or Dimension that the Devil won't try to corrupt their inhabitants in some way.

Animals were never meant to harm Humans on purpose. Some had been corrupted by the darkness and others harmed for protection of themselves and their own kind from Humans.

Before Humans evolved to higher intelligence, they attacked and killed animals mostly from fear of them. They used them for food and for their furs and skins. Animals were for Earth and not for Human consumption. No meat in any form or sea life or any other living being was meant for Human consumption. Humans were meant to consume plant life.

Not all of those less intelligent Humans killed animals for food or clothing however. Some did consume plant life. Others in different parts of Earth consumed animals due to the environment not providing enough plant life to sustain the Human life. They then turned to animals and/or sea life. The Humans that consumed animals and sea life evolved into unhealthy Humans susceptible to the eventual diseases, harsh weather, and environmental problems, and more. They evolved into more aggressive Humans in many ways. Their brains did not develop as healthily as it was meant to develop like the Humans that only consumed plant life.

Humans who consumed plant life only were more docile. They were peaceful and caring to themselves, to other Humans, and to animal life. They took care of Earth and the animals.

Humans that ate meat became aggressive to each other and to the other Humans who just ate plant life when they encountered those Humans due to moving into other parts of Earth. They were aggressive to the animals of all kinds as well. They showed no compassion and killed at will.

Animals developed a fear and aggression toward Humans because of how those Humans who ate meat were towards them. Animals had to defend themselves and their young. As animals evolved, they taught their young to defend themselves and the young watched the parents' actions.

As more time went on it just became second nature for some animals to defend themselves aggressively or to be aggressive towards Humans out of defense or fear of what the Humans might do to them. Other animals took the road of running away when they could. And others hid when they saw Humans not knowing if the Human was peaceful or not.

As animals evolved, they also developed a sense of danger. They sensed it from up close and from afar. They could smell danger and also feel it within themselves. Some animals were too trusting and others not trusting at all.

Due to some animals trusting, their species no longer exist. Some animals became extinct partly due to the weather, the lack of food on Earth, other aggressive species, but mostly due to Humans killing them off.

So, Humans were the reason for the fear and aggression of animals in the beginning here on Earth.

There were some species of animals that through time and evolvement became domesticated as in being pets for Humans. Dogs, cats, rodents, etc. However, even the domesticated animals at that point had the instinct of fear and aggression, and the sense of danger, yet could also be trusting, loving, and caring.

All animals were gifts from God to Earth and to Humans. They were to live peacefully together on this planet. And the domesticated animals were meant to give unconditional love to all. However, Humans managed to destroy that and still do sadly.

As Humans have a purpose on Earth, so do all animals have a purpose on Earth. A good and positive purpose.

What is the battle between "good" and "evil?"

Good is being a loving, joyous, helping, compassionate Human who believes in and worships God and rarely on purpose strays off the righteous path in life.

Evil is an angry, hate filled, revengeful, dangerous, and often violent Human whose purpose is to spread negativity and darkness throughout the world for all of their lives never serving or worshiping God, but who serves and/or worships the Devil.

So, if a Human who is good at times strays off the righteous path, then considered evil? No, not as long as they do not stay off the righteous path. There is something called repenting for a Human's sins. That is asking God for forgiveness for whatever non good the Human did. God forgives the "good" as long as that Human means their repentance and gets right back on the righteous path.

Humans are just that – Humans. God understands that life's circumstances can be quite rough and tough at times. It is during those times a Human can stay on the righteous path and trust God and have faith that whatever they are going through or dealing with will be worked out or end up in a positive way. Or, take the negative or dark path thinking that that is a better path because God doesn't love or care for them or even hear or answer their prayers.

God understands that the Devil loves to tempt the Humans that are "good" and try to lure them to his side of darkness and "evil." God understands that Humans have weaknesses due to whatever they are dealing with or going through such as grieving over the death of a loved one. The Devil loves to step in put all kinds of negative thoughts about God into the

Human's head. This is where the Human needs to have strong faith in God.

The Devil is strong. He will even send his Demons to do his dirty work. The Devil can never be trusted, and that is a fact. But God can always be trusted, and that is a fact. But in weak-willed times, the Human can certainly fall prey to the Devil. Even if the Human falls prey to the Devil, if the Human realizes that they have done that and repents asking for God's forgiveness and gets themselves back on the righteous path they are forgiven and once again considered "good."

Good is one Human helping another Human or other life form whether they are family, friends, or strangers. It's when the Human has full love in their heart and spreads that love throughout the world in their lives while on the Earthly plane. But there will always be **the battle between "good" and "evil"** because of the dark and negative temptations of the Devil in life. The Devil is relentless, and it takes a strong willed, strong faith in God Human to resist the temptations.

Evil is the dark and negative energy of the Devil, Demons, and Dark Energies/Entities who have successfully tempted and drawn a Human to their side through whatever means that they did. It could have been during a low period in the Human's life with the loss of a loved one, loss of a job, loss of a home, loss of finances, and more. The Devil tempts with negative words about God. And since the Human is experiencing those traumas in their life, they tend to believe the Devil thinking that God has forsaken them, and that God doesn't care about them or love them. Those are exactly the thoughts that the Devil puts in the Human's mind.

Evil is a Human that has been possessed by the darkness and does harm and kills other Humans and life forms on purpose.

The Human's mind has become corrupted by the darkness and they no longer operate as a loving and caring Human. Their mentally ill corrupted mind only knows how to spread negativity, hate, anger, violence, and more.

Evil are Humans who form negative and dark groups even calling those groups their Religion for the sole purpose to spread negativity, anger, hate, violence and more throughout the world. They purposely harm and kill because they have been possessed and/or corrupted by the Devil. They call themselves disciples of the Devil and only worship him. They hate God and all light beings. They hate all Humans that live for God and do "good" while on the Earthly plane.

These groups are always trying to recruit Humans dedicated to God and doing "good." These groups of Devil worshipers use dark magic to try to obtain what they want. They use rituals that purposely kill animals and even Humans using them as sacrifices to the Devil to get what they want or to show the Devil that they are on his side. These Devil worshiping groups are very dangerous. They even walk amongst, work with and for, and live around God worshiping Humans disguised at times to love and worship God. They do not love God. They only love the Devil.

The battle between "good" and "evil" has always existed and always will as long as the Devil and darkness exist.

Chapter 2

Religion

Humans created "Religion." When Humans formed, they grew and over time broke off into different groups. Some of these groups travelled to other lands on Earth procreating there and creating their lives. This happened all throughout time on Earth. Not all Humans travelled to other parts of Earth because Humans were formed all over Earth. So, some stayed where they were born, their place of origin.

All Humans believed in some higher power finding out that this was God. As intelligence developed in Humans, they looked deeper into how they came to be on this planet Earth. Many questions arose for them and they became very curious. This did not happen to all Humans, and of course, not at the same time. And it didn't happen all at once. This occurred as time went on.

For the Humans who felt a need to delve deeper into their existence, they started to try and connect by speaking to this unseen force or higher power or God. They would look up to the sky during the day and the stars during the night and ask questions. Some got answers. Those were the Humans who kept their born psychic abilities even though they had no idea that that was the reason they could see, hear, feel, or just know things. And for others it came in time.

Those Humans started speaking to other Humans and spreading the knowledge as it came to them. They even started writing down the information they were receiving. They became Humans of power. They became figureheads to other Humans. They were looked up to. And they were sought out for their knowledge and to answer questions that other Humans had. It all grew from there.

These "figurehead" Humans were those who started special groups for just this reason; to answer questions they got answers to from this higher power found out to be called God. The groups would unite from time to time for this very purpose and for guidance. This eventually became known as and called "Religion."

Because some of these figureheads' psychic abilities grew stronger and more powerful in receiving information from God they broke off and formed their own sect or Religion. They gave it their name but all with the bottom line of God as the source of knowledge and power and of creation of all things and of all life forms.

The questions and knowledge didn't stop there. It grew. More and more information was downloaded to these figureheads but not only to them but to other Humans who started being able to see, hear, feel, and know information from whom they knew as God.

Soon, there was the seeing of light beings whom they were told were called Angels. These light beings or Angels would reveal themselves to some Humans that were open to God or this higher power. Angels brought them knowledge. They also brought them protection from harm. They also showed Humans the way they needed to head in life, their paths.

As time went on, Archangels were revealed as were Guardian Angels. All revealing their purpose to the Humans and to Earth.

More and more Religious groups formed following what they believed and no longer believed of other groups or those other groups not being able to grow or provide growth of and into the Spiritual world. For some Humans, there was an unquenchable thirst for Spiritual knowledge.

Humans learned how to Meditate. This was the act of sitting quietly in a sacred place to them so as to speak to God and/or the Angels. They found that they not only could make contact with God and the Angels but with other beings, even ones from other Planets, Galaxies, and Dimensions as well as absorbing knowledge about that. This allowed these particular Humans to go off and form other Religious groups who believed in this and wanted to know more and practice it for themselves. A name was created for that Religious group related to their beliefs.

Not every group that formed throughout time called it Religion. But it still falls into that category in some way.

Then there were Humans that did not believe those Humans with the powers of psychic ability aka seers. They did not believe that Humans were able to chat with God, or see Angels and other light beings. Some were afraid and didn't want to know. They feared something bad would happen to them and/or their families if they were in contact with those light beings or God himself. They also didn't believe the seers because they themselves weren't experiencing the voice of God or seeing the light beings as the seers or psychics did. So, some Humans turned away from the seers with the psychic abilities feeling like they were something bad.

The Humans that did not want to or refused to join any Religious groups because they were afraid or didn't believe that there was a higher power or God eventually became known as Atheists. Atheists were those who believed there was some kind of higher power that created them but not called God. And no matter what the psychics said they still didn't believe. And they didn't believe in Angels or any light beings either.

According to where Humans lived on Earth, and their ethnicity the seers or psychics developed individual names for the work that they did. For instance, indigenous seers or psychics called themselves Shamans. Shamans were Spiritual practitioners, viewed as the bridge between the physical and Spiritual realms, using rituals, trances, and divination to communicate with Spirits, heal, and guide groups. Throughout time, Humans created titles for themselves such as Shaman, Prophet, Healer, Psychic, Medium, Seer, Intuitionist, Religious Leader, and more according to their abilities and beliefs.

Religion continued to grow, and powerful groups emerged almost forcing some Humans to join their Religion or else. Forcing Humans to join Religious groups is not from God but from the darkness, the Devil.

But some of these Religious groups became very powerful and worked with other powerful Humans throughout the Earth. They connected themselves with powerful rulers of countries in order to stay safe from being banished or killed. But there became unrest within their own Religious groups. Humans that rebelled were locked away, some tortured, and some killed.

Some of those powerful Religious groups at some point turned the corner to the dark side for power, money, protection from other Religious groups, and to stay alive during turbulent times as in battles and wars.

Some Religious groups were frowned upon for their beliefs because it wasn't what other Religious groups believed. The dark Religious groups plotted behind the backs of many other Religious groups forcing them to join their Religious group and belief, and if not, then destroying that group with force and possible death.

Dark and evil groups also formed throughout time. These were the Humans that did not believe in God, Angels or any other light being. They turned to worship the Devil aka Satan. They recruited and corrupted with the help of the Devil. They called themselves Religious but their belief and worship was to the Devil and all Dark Energies/Entities, even Demons. Their job was to corrupt with temptation as many Humans as they could.

Those dark groups also broke off into various sects because there became levels of darkness and corruption. As the Religious groups who worshipped and believed in God travelled throughout Earth recruiting for good, these dark groups also travelled throughout Earth recruiting for the Devil and trying to poison the minds of the Humans who followed the light – God. Some weak minded and weak-willed Humans did convert over to those dark groups and some did not. That battle still exists to this day on the Earthly plane.

Religion got very ugly throughout time and some of that still exists to this day. Not all, but some. There are some Religions to this day that are still quite powerful and wealthy, and they want it to stay that way. There is darkness behind them that they hide from the outside Humans who they call followers of their Religious group. Not all of these Religious groups are completely bad but corruption does still exist in some. Power and greed took over in some of these Religious groups long ago which is considered negative and even evil. Some of the Religious groups have a mixture of "good" and "evil' to this day.

The followers or congregation was and still is a mixture of God abiding Humans. Some are God abiding while they attend church services, and then outside of church at other times are corrupted in some way or live their lives corrupted. Some corruption is severe and some to a lesser degree. Hypocrisy exists with so many Humans who claim to be God loving and God abiding.

Not all followers of God who attend church or claim a Religion are corrupted. However, there is good and bad in all Religious groups. Always **the battle between "good" and "evil."**

Chapter 3

Church

First Religion and then Church. As religious groups formed, they would gather in all different places. Some places were outdoors while others indoors. Some of the indoor places were homes. The outdoors at times presented a problem for gathering because of the weather conditions. In some areas it was quite hot while in other areas it was quite cold. They also had to deal with rain, or snow, ice, any and all types of weather including severe heat. All this was depending on where on Earth they lived. Tents were put up to shield them from the sun and rain and other elements of the weather. But although that may have shielded them from some weather conditions, it was still either cold or hot inside. The beginning shelters had tops only called canopies and as they progressed canopies with sides were used called tents. Later on, as time and centuries went by more advanced systems were used as in heating and cooling devices.

Not only did the religious groups have to deal with weather but wildlife as well. Some places were unsafe to be outside. And they were not always safe inside the tents.

Tents also had to be expanded due to the religious groups following. Some groups grew faster and with more Humans than others.

The religious groups who held gatherings in their homes could only support a few members depending on the size of their home. The meetings or services were usually held at the home of the religious leader. Down the road as religion grew, so did the titles of the religious leaders depending on the sect of their religion. For example, Pastors and Priests were two titles of different sect religious leaders. Both of the Christian faith but Pastor of the Protestants and Priests of the Catholics.

As the homes became too small due to the growth of the religious groups, larger buildings were sought after for the sole purpose of the religious meetings or services. These buildings became known as Churches.

Churches, depending on the sect of the religious group, were designed and decorated to match their faith. Most of the Churches had a similar design and decoration. However, the beginning Churches had a very modest and simple design. Many barns were used as meeting places for their services until the congregation grew. Financial and material donations were eventually taken and this helped in the building of bigger and stronger buildings. And with this the insides began to be designed to be either simple or ornate depending on the religious group sect.

Each religion as they grew designed and decorated their Churches in a certain fashion. And depending on where on Earth the religious groups were, that played a part in the structure of the buildings and also its design. Depending on how much money the religious leaders were collecting from their congregations played a part in the size, design, and decoration of the structure of their Churches as well.

When different religious groups formed outside of Christianity, their buildings of prayer and worship looked different and were called by other names such as Temples.

To this day, there are Church structures of all sizes, designs, and decorations. They are located all over the Earth. However, less Humans worship in them due to their time schedules, beliefs, lifestyles, preferences, and more. But the devoted religious leaders still press on spreading the word of God and trying to keep and recruit more members to sustain and grow their congregations.

There are still some religious groups that hold their meetings or services from their homes or homes of others. They also rent locations to hold their meetings or services and also use those places to recruit new members into their religious beliefs.

Some religious groups go door to door of homes in an effort to recruit other Humans to join their religion. They hand out materials with religious information of their beliefs. They hold their meetings or services in a Church or Churchlike structure and even in their homes as well.

There are certain sect religious groups that are very powerful and rich and have enormous Churches and Cathedrals with a massive congregation and followers. Some of those powerful religions and religious leaders obtained status, power, and money by dark means and still do yet they claim to worship almighty God putting God first and in all things. A definite hypocrisy. Yet they and their Churches remain rich and powerful. Some, maybe most of them, joined forces with the dark side. Not everyone associated with those groups have corrupted to the dark side however, but many have, yet their faces, words, and actions hide the corruption and darkness.

Ah, **the battle between "good" and "evil."**

Chapter 4

Atheists

Why are there Humans who believe in religion? Why do Humans choose religion? Why do Humans and other life forms believe in God? These are some questions that could be asked as well. But let's talk about Atheism.

Atheists are Humans who believe there is no God. They do not believe what religion teaches nor do they believe what is written in the Bible. They do not believe there was a son of God known as Jesus.

Some Atheists do believe in a higher power but just do not know what or who that is. Some don't believe there is a who higher power or a what higher power. They feel something or someone brought them to Earth or something or someone created Humans. Some Atheists believe in the scientific explanation of Humans evolving from the ocean. And some Atheists believe the scientific explanation that Humans evolved from Apes or Apelike creatures.

Many Humans are Atheists because they ask the question that if there is a God, then why does God allow so much bad to happen on Earth. Why are there starving people and starving animals? Why is there crime? Why do Humans kill other Humans? Why do children die young or at birth? Why when something bad is happening God doesn't stop it or prevent it? The questions are endless from Atheists. If there really is a

God, then why does he allow the Devil to spread evil? All are good and valid questions.

The answer is that God gave Humans and other life forms free will. And the Devil, Demons, and Dark Energies/Entities roam the Earth, other Planets, Galaxies, and Dimensions spreading their disease of hatred and destruction tempting and possessing Humans and other life forms.

Also, Humans and other life forms leave the Earth, other Planets, Galaxies, and Dimensions when their time is up. Some have a shorter time given than others for many reasons. One reason is that a Soul wanted to reincarnate back to Earth, another Planet, Galaxy, or Dimension for a particular reason. Their reason may be for a short time to experience what they wanted to or to do what they needed to and then move back to the Universe.

When a Human or other life form's body dies at a young age for whatever way that the body dies be it by disease, at the hands of another Human or animal, at birth, etc., their time was up from wherever they were on Earth to move back to the Universe. God allows this because of free will and that the Soul had another purpose, wanted to leave, or needed to leave.

There is no time in the Universe as there is with Earth. So, when a Human or other life form ends at an early Earthly time/age, that has no relevance to the Universe. It is just that that particular Soul's time was up.

This is what is so hard for the Atheists to believe and accept. Religious and most Spiritual Humans feel differently with modifications to their beliefs. Some understand the reasons I just described and explained while others have their own beliefs of those questions from the Atheists.

Spiritual Humans are more open with broader understanding and belief in God and the Universe while many religious groups have a bit of a narrower view.

Humans and other life forms at times fall prey to the Dark Energies/Entities and their lives end. Some Humans have accidents that cause them to pass on. Some Humans and other life forms contract diseases and pass from that. Some Humans take their own lives. Some develop mental illness due to some type of trauma. And some of those mental illnesses are due to being corrupted by the dark side. But, even for those reasons, the Soul's time was up no matter what Earthly age they were.

Many Atheists are Earthly Scientists. Atheists do not believe in the supernatural, paranormal, or any Spiritual happenings. And if they do, then they are not true Atheists. And they should not live under that title.

Some Atheists do believe there is "God" so therefore, they are not true Atheists. They may say they believe in God but not the Devil or any other religious or Spiritual happening. Those are not true Atheists either.

Chapter 5

Cult versus The Occult

"Cult" - A system or group of people who practice excessive devotion to a figure, object, or belief system. They typically follow a charismatic leader or person who acts as a leader. The term Cult is commonly connected with highly unorthodox religious sects that take part in sinister practices and demonstrations.

"Occult" - Relates to magic, astrology, or any system claiming use or knowledge of secret or supernatural powers or agencies.

Cults start out with leaders who are possessed or corrupted by the Devil. They can even be Demons in disguise. Even if the Human leader of the Cult started out not corrupted by the darkness, they possess those overtones and soon thereafter become completely corrupted.

These are Humans or Demons that thirst for attention and need to make a mark in the world only using darkness as that mark. They are usually narcissists that need to be adored by other Humans but in a sick and twisted way. Their mind and way of thinking are severely corrupted with dark and negative visions. They enlist other Humans that are usually weak willed, their lives are in a bad way, or have been abandoned by family and/or friends. The Cult leader talks bad about God to the Humans making them believe that God doesn't love them and has abandoned them. They try to convince the Humans that they are there for them even if God isn't. They basically brain wash the Humans against God.

The Cult leader enlists other Humans and sends them out to grow the Cult community. The community usually ends up being filled with weak willed Humans who have been brainwashed to think that God hates them and will never help them and that the leader of the Cult is there for them, loves them, and will take care of them if they worship him.

The Cult leader wants to be or actually thinks that they are God or Godlike. They have sick minds and usually use their subjects which are other Humans, for their bidding which is always corrupt.

The Cult's mission is to spread their darkness to as many Humans as they can. They are a disease that infects society.

The Cult members who at some point think of trying to leave the group can find themselves stuck in the Cult. Their lives may even be threatened if they try to leave. And in some Cults, lives are definitely taken if they try to leave or challenge the Cult leader in any way.

When the Cult grows to a high number of members, a ranking is put in place. The Cult leader and the second in command, and a third in command. Almost like a King with his Kingdom, his trusted Guards, his Henchmen, and his subjects whom are beneath him.

The more power the Cult leader gets the more dangerous that Human becomes. He sends his leaders out with troops to enlist more Humans for the Cult. And darkness is used towards anyone who gets in the way.

If a Cult becomes examined by law enforcement, they may be forced to move their location. Some Cults branch off to other locations so that they can enlist more Humans into the Cult. The sickness grows and spreads like a disease.

The Devil supports these Cults and sends out Demons and Dark Energies/Entities to possess the Cult leaders and give them power to grow and spread the darkness. The Devil loves Cults and Cult leaders. The poor Humans in the Cult are usually just lost sheep that are now unable to escape even if they wanted to.

Cults may even kidnap people and hold them captive in their group forcing them to adapt to the Cult lifestyle and threaten them or their family if they leave.

Cult leaders often use drugs or medication in some way. And they may talk their group into taking drugs as well or even sneak the drugs into the drink and/or food. They many times use mind control substances to keep the group in line with what the Cult leader wants for that group.

Cults are quite sinister even though they may start out not so sinister. With more power the leader receives the more that that Human's mind goes haywire because they started out either being possessed by the darkness or are a Demon for the Devil.

Even if a Cult leader is not possessed by the darkness or is a Demon, they have some kind of emotional and/or mental disorder where the darkness is behind that. So, a Cult leader is not free and clear of the darkness. And this goes for others in the group that agree with the views of the Cult leader. Others in the group may be convinced by verbal mind control to believe what the Cult leader says is true. Or they may be drugged known or unbeknownst to them. Most of the time it is unbeknownst to them. The Cult leader's close ranking members may also be possessed by the darkness or are Demons. There is so much darkness to these Cults that the lines become blurred, but always in a negative way.

Cults can be very dangerous because what they want is never good. They may use the Cult group as a cover up for some kind of criminal activity stemming from stealing, to selling drugs, to Human trafficking. In any case, it is never good. And these activities may be unknown to the followers in the group. The Cult leader and his close members may keep that covered up with possible religious preaching to the group having them think that they are serving good and doing good in society when it is just the opposite.

Some Cult groups are darker than others but nevertheless lies are fed to the members having them think that the Cult leader is some kind of God. The more the Cult leader can control the members the more darkness he can spread.

Cult leaders are dangerous because they have mental issues of some sort with delusions of grandeur. They do not see or live life in reality. They live life from the mental images they receive from the darkness. And they are told to do things that are of the dark, and to spread that darkness. Some Cult leaders are told to become those leaders and to form a group with followers to spread the darkness, and for some, to the degree of evil.

Humans need to be aware of, and stay far away from Cults. And if they encounter a Cult leader or member of a Cult, do not get involved. If a Human accidentally gets involved in a Cult, because Cults disguise themselves as groups doing good for the world, get out fast if they can. Disassociate with them immediately.

Some Cults disguise themselves as religion while others disguise themselves as helping the world population or the planet Earth itself. It is easy to fall prey to Cults because they are good at lying. This is why when Humans fall prey to them and become a member of their group, it may be hard or almost impossible to escape. So, either the Human starts to agree with what the Cult believes and does what they are told, or before they become drugged, or threatened, they need to get out and as fast as they can.

Cult members that are able to escape the Cult may need professional help to undo the possible brainwashing that the Cult had done to them if they were a part of that group for a lengthy time. And they may even need to seek medical help as well in case they were drugged. Being able to escape a powerful Cult is no easy feat and can be very traumatic in all ways.

So, if a Human suspects that a group is a Cult or Cultlike, do not proceed with them. If the Human accidentally gets involved with them, get out fast.

The word **Occult** has negative overtones and some Humans associate and get confused with the Occult and a Cult.

Occult refers to beliefs and practices that are often seen as outside the scope of mainstream science and religion, encompassing supernatural phenomena, esoteric knowledge, and hidden wisdom. It involves concepts like magic, mysticism, Spirituality, and divination, often focusing on harnessing unseen powers or gaining access to secret knowledge. All of this is practiced with the light of God, Archangels, Angels, Guides, Ascended Masters, and other light beings. Very different from a Cult that only follows darkness.

There are groups that may form calling themselves Witches or practice certain Occult beliefs using magic spells and divination, and more to help or see the past, present, and future.

In the Occult, there are Psychics, Mediums, Tarot Readers, Pendulum users for divination, Spell Casters, and more but all are used for good and the purpose of helping others.

Spells may be cast to help someone attain love or love themselves. Spells may be cast to open doors to prosperity and abundance. These Spells are not evil but sent to the light for God and the other light beings to see and hear for the help of the Earthly plane Human(s). It is akin to prayer.

There are Spells done to banish the darkness or evil in some way or form which is still a good thing. It is within the realm of light and not dark.

The Occult works with crystals and stones for healing, protection, etc. Some Humans buy and sell beautiful pieces. Some create beautiful jewelry out of those crystals and stones.

The Occult uses music to soothe and heal Humans, and to send love to the Universe. Some groups may gather for a healing session as sound can heal, or to send thanks to the Universe for all the blessings received. Music may be played using various musical instruments and even bowls that create sound to connect with the ancestors and/or to thank them.

Meditation is something that falls into the category of the Occult. Meditation is practiced to help a Human calm their entire being releasing the stresses of the day. It may be used to connect with a Human's higher self or to connect with God or other light beings. Some Humans meditate to connect with their Guides to obtain answers that they seek. Meditation is a great tool for Humans in so many ways.

Astral Traveling is another practice of Humans that falls into the category of the Occult. Astral Traveling can be tricky though and a bit dangerous as it takes the Human's Spirit out of the body to travel to other places. While Astral Traveling, the Human travels in the in-between world where all the Spirits reside. This can be dangerous because that plane has good Spirits and not good Spirits and even evil Spirits. Those dark Spirits can attach themselves to the Human and travel back to the Earthly plane with the Human.

So, Astral Traveling is not a good idea especially for those who do not have the full knowledge about that practice. It can be a beautiful and exciting experience yet it can have just the opposite.

A Human should always take precaution by visualizing themselves tethered to the item they are on whether a chair or a bed or even the floor. This way the Spirit can always get back into the physical body. And just as important is to become completely knowledgeable of Astral Travel before purposely practicing it. I use the word purposely because there are times that the Spirit will Astral Travel on its own without the Human knowing it. If a Human does not have an understanding of Astral Travel or ever heard of it, they may feel as if they left their body but not know what really happened to them. This could be exciting to them or a scary experience.

Now, here's where it gets tricky with the Occult. Unfortunately, there may be groups formed for the purpose of darkness. They may worship the Devil. Their beliefs are askew. But those Humans are already corrupted by the Devil, Demons, and/or Dark Energies/Entities. Their beliefs are far from what the beliefs are of the Occult which is of the light and serve God.

These dark Devil worshiping groups use magic and spells but of the very darkest of dark. They cast spells to try to hurt, torment, torture, and even try to kill. They sacrifice poor loving animals and even Humans for the Devil. Their minds are completely overtaken by the dark.

The even scarier part is that these Humans may look like every day Humans living their lives with no one suspecting their dark practices or that they are of the Devil and worship him. These dark groups lean more towards a Cult than the Occult. The only difference is that these dark groups use black magic, dark spells, and make sacrifices.

This is why Humans associate the Occult with a Cult. There is that confusion. But the Occult is, other than the dark groups I mentioned, of the light. And Cults are of the dark.

This is definitely **the battle between "good" and "evil."**

Chapter 6

Angels

There are Archangels, Guardian Angels, Angels. Angels are light beings discharged to Earth and other Planets, Galaxies, and Dimensions to help and protect Humans and other life forms. They are beautiful and peaceful light beings.

Archangels

Archangels are Angels of high rank. They are viewed as leaders or messengers of God. Archangels are at the top of the Angelic hierarchy. Here are some of God's Archangels to help Humans through their lives of ups and downs, good and bad, and from darkness to light.

Archangel Michael: Archangel Michael is the highest and strongest Archangel whom in times of need aids life forms in battles of physical, emotional, or mental trials. When a Human or other life form cries out for help to Archangel Michael, he comes to their aid to fight or help them fight whatever they are battling.

As Humans, there will be times of hardship whether it be emotional, mental, or physical. There will be times when Humans do not have the strength to fight situations they may be dealing with. This is the time to call on Archangel Michael for help in whatever the Humans are facing in their lives. Archangel Michael can hear whether he is called within the mind or actual use of voice.

Archangel Gabriel: Archangel Gabriel is considered the Messenger of God. He is dispatched to give important messages from God to Humans and other life forms.

So, if and when Archangel Gabriel shows up in your life whether in a dream, meditation, or just in front of a waking Human, they should pay attention because he has an important message for that Human straight from God. And Archangel Gabriel can take a message from a Human straight to God.

Archangel Raphael: Archangel Raphael is the Healer. When a Human or other life form needs healing physically, emotional, or mentally, he is the Archangel to call upon for the healing.

Many times, throughout the Humans' lives, they face emotional, mental, and physical illness. Even if a Human believes completely in scientific medicine, they may also have a Spiritual side and Archangel Raphael is the one to call upon for help with their issues. Ask him to send and surround you inside and outside with his green healing light.

And Archangel Raphael is also known as the Archangel of Marriage. He is a powerful ally in helping Humans find their marriage partners. So, if a Human is feeling like they could use help in this area, then they should call upon Archangel Raphael for help.

Archangel Uriel: Archangel Uriel is the Archangel of Truth and Wisdom. He helps guide Humans towards enlightenment and helps them navigate challenges with faith and clarity.

There will be times when Humans face certain challenges in their lives be it with health, finances, relationships, career, faith, and more. At and during those times Archangel Uriel would be the one to call upon for help.

Archangel Azrael: Archangel Azrael is one of the top Archangels. He helps take the Souls away from a deceased body. When a Soul's time is up on Earth, on other Planets, in other Galaxies, and other Dimensions, God dispatches Archangel Azrael to go and collect the Soul from the deceased body. Archangel Azrael can only take that order from God. He is also sent as a source of comfort to Humans and other life forms who are grieving the loss of a loved one be it another Human or beloved pet.

So, if Archangel Azrael happens to show up in a Human's dream or meditation, there is no need for alarm as it might just be because they are going through a very emotionally difficult time or grieving over a loss, and Archangel Azrael shows up to give them comfort.

Archangel Jophiel: Archangel Jophiel is an Archangel known as the "beauty of God." She emanates divine wisdom and inspiration, and transforms negative emotions into positive energy. Her energy encourages both inner and outer beauty, helping people cultivate not just physical grace but also a deeper sense of spiritual self. Archangel Jophiel also changes chaos to calm. She can help you manifest beauty into your life. She can also help guide thoughts towards a more positive direction and love.

Archangel Haniel: Archangel Haniel is known for joy, happiness, and fulfillment. She can help guide Humans towards joy and fulfillment by helping them find happiness within themselves and connect with or connect deeper with God. Archangel Haniel helps Humans follow their passion and find enjoyment in present moments.

So, when a Human is feeling unhappy for whatever reason that is, or cannot seem to find happiness or joy in their lives, they should call upon Archangel Haniel for help.

Archangel Metatron: Archangel Metatron is a scribe to God and guide to Humans and other life forms. He is the spokesperson of God. Archangel Metatron gives Humans and other life forms a way to communicate with God so that he can hear their thoughts and prayers. He records the sins, choices, decisions, and merits of Humans and other life forms. Archangel Metatron also helps Humans and other life forms with their journey and understanding their purpose.

Many times, Humans ask the question of what is their purpose. If the Human is struggling in that arena, they should call upon Archangel Metatron to help them find clarity and answers.

Archangel Chamuel: Archangel Chamuel helps bring peace to the world. He helps Humans find peace within themselves, their relationships, and offers guidance for healing. He helps with overcoming difficult situations and is associated with love.

Archangel Ariel: Archangel Ariel is known for being the angel of nature. She oversees the protection and healing of animals and plants, as well as the care of the Earth's, other Planets', and other Dimensions' elements. And is believed to punish those who harm God's creation.

It is best for Humans to be kind to each other and to all the animals God gave Humans to enjoy on Earth. Work with Archangel Ariel to help keep all life forms associated with Earth including plant life alive and growing to sustain Earth.

Archangel Raziel: Archangel Raziel helps to unlock creativity or enhance your spiritual path or abilities. He helps Humans and other life forms understand any complex situation they need help solving. Archangel Raziel provides clarity to help you find your true purpose and path in life. He will unlock the door to the laws of the Universe, Spirituality, and knowledge in general. Archangel Raziel's energy will help provide a more thorough understanding and deeper wisdom.

Archangel Jeremiel: Archangel Jeremiel is known as the Angel of Hope and Transition. He guides Humans and other life forms through challenging and difficult times. He helps them to find new direction and purpose in life. And he is known to change challenges into opportunities for growth. He opens Humans and other life forms to hope. Archangel Jeremiel is also known for emotional and physical healing.

It is easy for Humans to lose faith and hope at times during their lives. A Human should call upon Archangel Jeremiel when they are experiencing this as he can help guide them back to faith and hope. He can also help them when a Human is going through transitions in their life. And all Humans experience transitions in one way or another.

Archangel Sandalphon: Archangel Sandalphon acts as a conduit between Humans and other life forms and God. He is known to gather prayers and presents them to God. Also, helps Humans and other life forms understand their Soul's lessons. Archangel Sandalphon is known as the Angel of Music and Prayer helping Humans and other life forms use music to communicate with God in prayer. He is known to join forces with other Archangels such as Archangel Michael to fight the Devil and his Dark Energies/Entities in the Spiritual realm.

Guardian Angels

Guardian Angels are Angels assigned to guide and protect a particular Human or other life form, group, or nation. They help them to avoid Spiritual and physical dangers.

Guardian Angels can be Angels, passed over loved ones or friends who have returned to the Earthly plane to watch over a particular Human or other life form on other Planets, Galaxies, and Dimensions. They can be complete strangers dispersed by God to protect and guide a particular Human or other life form.

Guardian Angels act as protectors steering the Human or other life form away from danger and harm both physically and Spiritually.

They are also seen as Guides in helping the Human or other life form make good choices for their life – ones that are pleasing to God.

Guardian Angels act as a go between with God praying for their needs on behalf of the Human or other life form.

A Guardian Angel is assigned by God or chooses a particular Human or other life form for their entire life on Earth or on another Planet, in another Galaxy, or Dimension. They try to steer the Human or other life form away from danger. They can call on other Angels to assist them if needed.

Guardian Angels work through the Human's or other life form's intuition to steer them away from danger or onto a different or better path in life. They try to help them in whatever way they can without going against free will. They are also known to send Angels in Human or other life form forms to help.

A Human or other life form can speak with their Guardian Angel. They can ask a name or any question. However, only the Humans or other life forms with a high vibration will be able to hear and/or see them. But the answers can be revealed in dreams and signs and symbols.

When the life of the Human or other life form is up, the Guardian waits until the body is deceased and the Soul leaves the deceased body. At that point the Guardian Angel will return to the Universe to either be dispatched once again for a new life to protect and guide or another path for that Guardian Angel is taken. If they were once Human or other life form, they may decide to return to Earth again as a Human or go to another Planet, another Galaxy, or Dimension unless God has other plans for them.

All Humans and other life forms have a Guardian Angel until their physical body ceases to exist.

Angels

Angels are Spiritual beings who serve as messengers and servants of God. They possess intelligence, emotions, and wills. They are a heavenly or supernatural being without a physical body.

Angels are messengers between God and Humans and other life forms. They can have a Humanlike appearance but with wings like a bird. And some Angels may have a silhouette of a Human but with wings yet not have actual clear facial features of a Human.

Angels can be different sizes. They can be bright white light or they can be darker in shade as in gray. They may show an appearance of wearing a white or gray gown or robe.

They dwell in Heaven and are protectors of the righteous. They worship and serve God and are not to be worshipped.

Angels can walk the Earth, be on other Planets, in other Galaxies, and Dimensions. When on Earth they can be in Human form not known or seen as an Angel. However, these Angels in Human form may show signs of this radiant energy, extraordinary kindness, high intuitiveness, intense empathy, having a natural healing presence, and a deep sense of being guided towards the right path.

When Angels are walking Earth or on another Planet, in another Galaxy, or Dimension, they have been dispatched by God to be there. They are needed by God to either protect someone or something, get an important message to someone or something, or spread the word of God.

Angels in their natural form can pass through solid walls and structures. They can pass through glass windows that are not open. They can pass through doors that are not open. They can come through ceilings and floors. They do not need an opening to enter a structure or exit one. Angels can walk, float, and fly. They can just materialize out of thin air. They move about at will. Angels can touch a Human or other life form without the Human or other life form knowing it or feeling it. And they can touch a Human or other life form and be felt.

Some Humans feel that Angels are mythical creatures. They are not. Mythical creatures would be Unicorns, Werewolves,

Hydras, etc. Angels are real and not mythical. They are also not creatures. They are supernatural beings that are dispatched by God to help the Humans and other life forms on Earth, on other Planets, in other Galaxies, and Dimensions.

Angels can be anywhere they need to be. And they can be sent anywhere that they are needed. They can be sent to comfort a Human that is dealing with grief over the passing of a loved one be it another Human or a beloved pet. Angels can be sent to intervene in a dangerous situation. Or they can be sent to stop something bad from happening. Angels are also known to visit Humans that do wrong and convince them to turn themselves into authorities by touching their emotions. Some Angels are sent to ward off evil. There are many reasons Angels are dispatched to Earth, other Planets, Galaxies, and Dimensions.

Keep in mind though that Angels cannot interfere with a Human's free will. And although Angels can stop some earthquakes, hurricanes, fires, or worse from happening, or try to lessen their effects, they cannot force a Human out of an area if the Human's free will is to stay there. Also, when those disasters do strike, they are beyond the Angels. That means that those disasters were powerfully sent from the darkness or God has allowed them for a reason that was necessary.

Angels are beautiful and loving. Their job is to help Humans and other life forms on Earth, on other Planets, in other Galaxies, and Dimensions in whatever way they are dispatched. They serve and worship God and God alone.

Although Angels are beautiful peaceful light beings that serve God, they too get caught up **in the battle between "good" and "evil"** because they are dispatched by God to come to Earth to defend and protect Humans and other life forms from succumbing to the darkness.

Chapter 7

Guides

Guides, also known as Spirit Guides, are not the same as Archangels, Guardian Angels, or Angels. Whereas, Guardian Angels come to Earth, go to other Planets, to other Galaxies, and to other Dimensions, to be with a specific Human or other life form from their birth and stay throughout their entire lives until the Human's or other life form's body dies/ceases to exist, the Guides do not do that. At that point of the Human's body or other life form's body ceasing to exist, the Guardian Angel along with Archangel Azrael takes the Soul back to Heaven/the Universe.

The Guides are sent to Humans and other life forms at the beginning of their life to help them on their journey while on the Earthly plane, on other Planets, in other Galaxies, or Dimensions until the Human or other life form ceases to exist. While there is only one Guardian Angel throughout the Human's or other life form's life, there can be many Guides helping them along.

Guides can be sent for specific reasons. To be with the Human or other life form helping them through and steering them away from danger or wrong turns and getting them back on the right path.

Guides can come for seasons in a Human's or other life form's life. When the reason a Guide was with them is completed, that Guide may leave and be replaced by another Guide of a higher level for that Human's or other life form's next chapter.

A Guide can be a loved one who had passed away at some point. Or can be a complete stranger who was dispatched by God to come back to the Earthly plane to help and guide for a specific reason or timeframe of need.

A Guide can be someone from a far-off past who was here on Earth at some point and now either wanted to be a Guide or was commissioned by God. A loved one who had passed over can ask to come back and be a Guide for a living loved one be it a family member or friend they left behind on the Earthly plane or to a complete stranger. And a Guide can be an Alien from another Planet, Galaxy, or Dimension. Ascended Masters can act as Guides as well.

Humans and other life forms can have more than one Guide at the same time. This is because in that particular chapter of the Human's or other life form's life, it may take more than one Guide.

Humans and other life forms can connect with their Guides. For Humans it can be done in silence or in meditation. It might not be easy for those who aren't open or fully open to the Spiritual world but can with practice and time connect. Although they do not really have names, they can give you a name to call them because that might make the Human feel more comfortable and not be afraid or feel less afraid to connect with them.

Guides can be asked anything and are willing to help as that is their job. They do vibrate at a very high Spiritual level so that is why the average Human cannot see, hear, speak with, or feel them. But again, with practice in the Spiritual world of connecting with them it can be done and answers to questions can be received.

Guides want and would love their Humans and other life forms to connect with them. If a Human cannot connect with them Spiritually, they can just ask in their mind or use their voice and ask out loud for a sign that their Guides or Guide is there. The Guide(s) can also give a sign as an answer to a question a Human might have for them. There is always a way to connect with the Guides.

Now, since Humans and other life forms have free will, it can be a bit tricky for the Guide. They do everything they can to deter or steer a Human or other life form out of harm's way, or to take another path, or make other decisions that would be best and right for them. However, with that free will, the Human or other life form can completely miss the sign given to them or other communication the Guide(s) tried to get through to them.

This can happen especially if a Human is dealing with fear or an emotional situation that causes their mind to be preoccupied or closed off. And Guides cannot make or force a Human or other life form to do something or go in a direction they choose not to. This is what is a bit frustrating for the Guides. However, the Guides get to work on righting some of those wrongs or steering them back on the right path. But Humans and other life forms can be quite resistant.

Depending on the situation, the Guide(s) will try to help the Human or other life form to stay away from the darkness and temptations of the Devil, and to regain their right way in life if they have veered off the correct path. Guardian Angels also have a bit of a hard time with some Humans and other life forms in trying to keep them from harm or harmful situations or making harmful decisions, but they never stop trying to help.

Guides, as you can tell by what you just read, are in **the battle between "good" and "evil."**

Chapter 8

The Devil

The Devil is many things and can be many things. He has many names and many faces. He goes by several names - Devil, Satan, Lucifer, Lord of the Darkness, the Anti-Christ, and more. And all things related to him are evil. The Devil is all darkness and the ultimate darkness. He is menacing and controls the Demons and Dark Energies/Entities in the ethers and on Earth, on other Planets, and in other Galaxies, and Dimensions. His sole purpose is to wreak havoc, corrupt, possess, torment, torture, destroy, kill, and more wherever he goes or have his followers help or do it for him.

The Devil can take on any form, almost like a chameleon. He is a shapeshifter changing from one Human form or thing to another. He can transform himself to look exactly like another Human that already exists on the Earthly plane. And he can do this on other Planets, in other Galaxies, and Dimensions with the life forms that live there.

The Devil takes pleasure in harming and/or killing. And he takes pleasure when a Human or other life form harms and/or kills themselves or others. The Devil is behind everything dark and evil.

As God dispatches Angels to help, protect, and heal, the Devil dispatches his Demons and Dark Energies/Entities to corrupt, possess, torment, torture, harm, and kill. There is no Human or other life form that is completely safe from the Devil.

The Devil looks for the weak and innocent no matter the age. He seeks out Humans and other life forms who are physically ill or with weak wills. He looks for the Humans that are down and out. He looks for the emotionally weak or lost. They are easier to tempt to the dark side. He searches out Humans and other life forms that have no place to go. The Devil is always searching and searching and tempting and tempting. He loves to temp the grieving Humans who have lost loved ones because they are quite vulnerable at that point. He loves to tempt the Humans that are financially struggling. He loves to tempt the Humans that are wealthy so he can turn them greedy. There is no end to the Devil's temptations. The more he can persuade to his side the more he loves it.

The Devil is dark in color. He is shadow dark and can be black just like the paint color black. He is black and dark through and through. He has no heart to feel. He does not want to feel. But he can feel something and that is joy when another joins him on the dark side. But that joy is for dark and not the joyous feeling a Human or other life form can experience.

The Devil is quite powerful, however not more powerful than God. The Devil steps in when his Demons or Dark

Energies/Entities cannot convince a Human or other life form to the dark side. He steps in when the Human or other life form is too strong willed for the Demons or Dark Energies/Entities to conquer. Much of the time the Devil will seal the deal but not all of the time. He decides whether or not that Human or other life form is worth it at that time. And he might revisit them at a later date. The Devil never gives up especially when he wants a particular Human or other life form.

The Devil loves a challenge. He loves to tempt the strong and strong-willed Humans and other life forms. He will use anything to tempt them. He studies them to try to find their weaknesses and then tempts there.

For easier prey, he sends his Demons and Dark Energies/Entities. They have levels of evil. So, before he steps in, he will dispatch a high-level Demon or Dark Energy/Entity to do the job when they are up against a strong Human or other life form. If the high-level Demons or Dark Energies/Entities still cannot seal the deal then he will step in. And the Devil will determine at that point whether to pursue the Human or other life form or wait for a time that they are at an emotional or physical low point and then try the strike again. There is nothing the Devil won't do or try. He derives pleasure from the hunt, the temptation, the corruption, the torment, the torture, and even death of a Human or other life form. He is the ultimate evil.

Some Humans do not believe in the Devil or believe the Devil exists. But the Devil is alive and well.

When bad or terrible things happen, they do not say it is because of the Devil. They may come up with another excuse or have some scientific reason for the happening. The Devil loves when Humans do not believe in him because it gives him an excuse to aggravate those Humans even more. To the Devil, those Humans are less intelligent even though they may be quite intelligent.

Some Humans believe that when something bad happens it is God's will. Or, the Humans who had something bad happened got their Karma or brought their situation on themselves. The Devil laughs at this reasoning. The Devil knows that God does not cause or present bad things to Humans or other life forms. And the Devil laughs at the Karma reason as well.

The Devil purposely harasses Humans for the sheer purpose of enjoyment. He loves to see them unhappy, or angry, or upset, or worried, or stressed. He loves to cause arguments and disagreements between them. Those are negatives to a Human and therefore a positive to the Devil. The more Humans feel or experience those emotions the more he loves it. And the more the Devil will provide.

The Devil loves when Humans grieve. It weakens their ability to fight off negative and bad. This is when the Devil swoops in and tries to sway those Humans to the other side by making them think that God allowed the situation to happen and that God doesn't care or love them. He loves when Humans blame God for the bad that happens. Anything that a Human feels that is negative towards God and other light beings the Devil loves. And the Devil will continue his lies to Humans in attempt to divide them from and/or keep them from God.

For some Humans, they will finish their lives out against God blaming him for things that happened to them during their lives on the Earthly plane. Any Human against God is a win for the Devil. This is his mission. And he won't stop until he corrupts all life forms on Earth, other Planets, in other Galaxies, and Dimensions. It's **the battle between "good" and "evil."**

Chapter 9

Demons

Demons are the disciples of the Devil. As Angels strictly take orders from God, Demons strictly take orders from the Devil.

Demons are actual physical bodies that walk amongst Humans corrupting whomever they can or fall prey to them. They tempt as the Devil tempts. Demons are dispersed by the Devil whom is the darkest of all. They are very cunning and can take Human form on its own. A Demon does not enter a Human's body but tortures physically, emotionally, and mentally the Human as a standalone entity.

A Demon comes already in physical form disguised as anyone or anything. Demons are the physical form that can be touched and seen that can physically harm Humans as it bodily tortures. A Demon is a tangible being.

Demons are disbursed by the Devil to recruit for the dark side. If they cannot sway or pull the Human to the dark side, they will then tempt harder. If the Human is still resistant the Demon will turn to mental, emotional, and even physical torture of the Human.

Demons love to frighten and scare all Humans and other life forms. They derive pleasure from this as the Devil does. They have no compassion for any Human or other life form. They open portals and find open portals to enter the Earthly plane and travel to other Planets, Galaxies, and Dimensions to corrupt, scare, torment, torture, and more.

Demons not only walk and corrupt on Earth, they can travel to other Planets, Galaxies, and Dimensions. There are many Demons. And the frightening part is that they can be completely disguised as any living being just to tempt and corrupt. It is their sole mission to do that.

Demons can be disguised as a family member, friend, colleague, or any other life form that a Human will trust and invite into their life. They do this to get close to the Human and then begin their temptations and corruption.

They may invite a Human to join a group and it turns out to be a cult or religious group with a cult leader whom is another Demon or a Human possessed by a Dark Energy/Entity.

Demons kidnap children and adult Humans; any age really. Many serial killers are Demons or Humans possessed by a Dark Energy/Entity.

There are degrees of Demons. They may be slightly deranged to severely deranged. The slightly deranged Demon will tempt Humans and scare them but not physically harm them. They like to torture Humans emotionally and mentally. The severely deranged Demon will torture and kill Humans and other life forms just for fun. They do not have a need to try to sway the Human to the dark side. They derive pleasure from harming all life forms. These are the most dangerous Demons. They have no compassion for any living being. A Human would never be able to talk or fight their way out of the severely deranged Demon's clutches.

Demons can be quite strong depending on their physical appearance. And a Demon does not have to be a male gender. They can be female as well. And they can appear as any age.

A Demon's appearance can be quite beautiful or quite ugly and scary. It depends on what the Demon's mission and order is from the Devil. When an order is given by the Devil, the Demon will then appear in the form that will work best for them to obtain what they want or are missioned for. Keep in mind that the Devil is behind all evil.

If a Human is experiencing demonic activity or being tormented by a Demon, they should call upon the Spiritual force of Archangel Michael as he is the Angel who leads the forces of Heaven to battle Demons, even the Devil.

As Aliens walk amongst Humans on Earth, so do Demons.
As long as Demons walk amongst the Humans and other life forms, there will always be **the battle between "good" and "evil."**

Chapter 10

Dark Energies/Entities

Dark Energies/Entities entails those passed on forms that have wreaked havoc on the Earthly plane and on other Planets, in other Galaxies, and Dimensions. There is no Planet, Galaxy, or Dimension that houses only the dark and negative. Those Dark energies can travel all throughout the Universe stopping and wreaking havoc wherever they go. They are energies and have no physical form unless they inhabit a Human or other life form. They are unlike Demons who actually already have a physical body.

Dark Energies/Entities can enter a Human body and overtake the physical, emotional, and mental aspects of the Human as well. Dark Energies/Entities float everywhere. They can inhabit a home and wreak havoc by moving physical objects and also destroying them. They can pass through physical solid structures and even enter the physical body possessing the Human. Dark Energies/Entities can enter a healthy Human body and corrupt the emotions and mind, and can actually destroy the physical body from within to the point of severe illness to near or actual death.

Dark Energies/Entities can travel through open portals on the Earthly plane and throughout the Universe. They travel to other Planets, Galaxies, and Dimensions spreading their evil.

Dark Energies/Entities love to frighten Humans at night when the Human goes to bed. When the Human falls into the in-between state of sleep which is not fully asleep nor fully awake, the Dark Energy/Entity attacks the Human. The in-between state is where all Spirits roam good and bad. A Dark Energy/Entity in this Human's stage of sleep will reveal themselves to a certain degree enough to frighten the Human. They can even physically attack them. This can cause a Human to fear going to sleep or even passing by or entering the room where the Dark Energy/Entity was seen and felt.

Dark Energies/Entities can also enter into a Human's dreams when they are fully asleep. They can cause nightmares and emotional and mental trauma. This can cause a Human to experience sleep deprivation from a non-restful sleep to not going to sleep at all for long periods of time due to fear of experiencing the trauma.

The Dark Energies/Entities can be the scariest to encounter because they aren't always seen. Most of the time they aren't seen at all but their presence can be felt by a Human, although the Human might not know that a Dark Energy/Entity is actually there, but the Human may feel a dark presence around them or in the room or even outside.

Dark Energies/Entities are the cause of mental illness outside of an accidental trauma to the brain. But if you look deeper, most likely some darkness caused the trauma to the brain in the first place by causing that accident to happen in whatever way it happened to the Human. Mental illness in a Human can go from mild to severe inflicting violence upon themselves and/or others. This will depend on what the Dark Energy/Entity is doing to the Human and for how long.

Some Humans may recover from their mental illness if the Dark Energy/Entity leaves the body before permanent damage has been done to that Human. Most Dark Energies/Entities like to keep the Human in torment for their entire lives. They can even enter a Human baby in a mother's womb and disrupt the brain and development before the baby is born. Then when the baby is born there already are mental and/or physical issues.

Dark Energies/Entities can be very sinister. They sneak up on Humans. At times they watch and watch, and study a Human before they make their attack. They decide whether or not they want to cause trauma to the Human or just scare them in some way. They decide what trauma they want to cause and for how long. This will depend on their orders from the Devil. And at times, they do not need orders from the Devil. They can be free to roam around spreading evil. They watch and follow the Human observing their every move, even when they sleep at night.

Dark Energies/Entities love a challenge, and if a Human is too easy to possess, they might not bother. This will depend on the actual Dark Energy/Entity or if they have orders from the Devil towards that particular Human. Some love to pounce on the weak while others love or need a challenge and will go after all the strong willed and strong in faith Humans.

Dark Energies/Entities will attack Humans going through grief or having difficulty in life in some way. For example, if it is a financial difficulty the Human is dealing with, the Dark Energy/Entity might enter that Human's life and cause it to be prolonged or cause a slight financial hardship to turn severe. This could cause a Human to head into depression, where the

Dark Energies/Entities love Humans to be, or cause the Human to harm themselves or to do something they would never do as in steal money. This is just one example of what Dark Energies/Entities look for in Humans and love to torment them with. The financial problem of a Human causes a weakness that the Dark Energy/Entity pounces on and can take to a whole other level for as long as that darkness wants.

Dark Energies/Entities love when a Human is grieving. It opens the door for them to cause the grief to last longer or never leave the Human causing that grief to be a daily torment and torture to the Human's emotional and mental state. And with some Humans, this can turn to depression.

They can actually cause depression in Humans. They attack the Human's emotional and mental state. One minute a Human can be feeling wonderful and happy and having a good time and then an emotional attack takes place and they all of a sudden feel depressed. The Dark Energy/Entity causes the Human to start thinking sad or bad thoughts. These thoughts can come out of nowhere with nothing triggering them. Or they can be triggered by something the Human sees or does. And that trigger was set by the Dark Energy/Entity as they may have put those triggers in the Human's path whether in their home, a store, or out and about somewhere. A Human can be driving or riding in a vehicle and start to feel depressed out of the blue.

Dark Energies/Entities can keep a Human in depression and cause the depression to deepen. If the Human becomes diagnosed by a doctor and given medication, the Dark Energy/Entity can cause that medication to not work, or to work at first and then not work properly or at all at some point.

What the Dark Energy/Entity wants is for that Human to become severely depressed at some point where it affects their entire life in some way in a very negative way. They want the depression so deep within a Human that nothing helps them, and they try to or actually take their own life.

The really scary part about Dark Energies/Entities is that a Human most of the time doesn't see them coming. They strike Humans at will. Frighteningly, they can enter right into a Human's body and/or mind. They can completely take over that Human in whatever way they want to and for how long they want to. However, if the Human body ceases to exist, then the Dark Energy/Entity immediately leaves looking for another to torment and torture because that's fun for them.

Not every Human will be bothered by Dark Energies/Entities but I say most will in some way whether slightly or severely. The weak are very vulnerable and easier to be overtaken by the darkness. And the very strong are enticing to the darkness. I don't think a Human can live out their life on the Earthly plane without incident in some way from a Dark Energy/Entity, a Demon, or the Devil. When I say not every Human will be bothered by the darkness, I mean they might not know that their low times or problems in life stemmed from some kind of darkness attacking. They may not suffer the torment and torture like some other Humans may. But no Human will leave this planet unscathed.

Humans can try to overpower Dark Energies/Entities and Demons but extremely hard to overpower the Devil. Resistance in all forms must be taken. Faith is the key. But the more faith, the harder the darkness will try. The Devil wants one thing, and that's to corrupt all Humans and take control spreading evil all over Earth and beyond. And that's because the Devil hates God and all whom and what God loves, and all who love God.

The Devil has no power with or over God, nor do Dark Energies/Entities and Demons. Dark Energies/Entities and Demons belong to the Devil. He uses them in any way that will work or just to emotionally torment and torture a Human. When a Human is tormented and/or tortured long enough in any way, the Human becomes weak in all ways, and therefore easier to be taken control of and corrupted by the dark. The Human loses their ability to fight physically, emotionally and/or mentally.

Dark Energies/Entities can cause a person to go insane. A healthy Human can become unhealthy. They can cause an emotionally and mentally stable Human to become unstable, and can cause illness to the physical body to erupt as well.

Dark Energies/Entities tempt, torment, and torture until they weaken the Human in some way. They love to overtake the strong and devour the weak. They will use money, status, and power as temptations, even fame. All that looks mighty good to the greedy, a poor and maybe starving Human or struggling Human family. There is no end to the temptations of the darkness.

Strong faith in God is the best armor. Staying on the right or righteous path is a must. It is not to say that a Human has to be religious or join a religion unless that is what the Human wants, but strong faith in and love for God, is what is needed. Call upon God for strength and ask for Archangel Michael whom is the Angel of Protection. There are also crystals and stones that can be used for protection. There is good armor at your disposal. Know that God loves all Humans and other life forms, and is there at any moment of need. Just call upon God.

There is always going to be **the battle between "good" and "evil"** for Humans and other life forms while living on the Earthly plane. And this goes for other life forms on other Planets, in other Galaxies, and Dimensions.

Chapter 11

Darkness & Evil Hates Humans

Darkness and Evil comes in many forms. It can come in the form of another Human. It can come in the form of an animal. It can come in the form of an Alien. It can come in the form of insects. It can come in any form that breathes life.

Darkness is the Devil. Darkness is Demons. Darkness is Dark Energies/Entities. The Devil has many faces and appearances. The Devil can shapeshift into anyone or anything he wants to. The Devil is the head of darkness and evil. There is no worse than the Devil. He controls all the Demons and Dark Energies/Entities. And he controls many Humans on this Earthly plane.

The Devil can corrupt a life form during the forming of that life while still inside the mother figure whether Human, animal, or other life form that births from their body. He corrupts the brain as it forms. He can also cause a malfunction in the actual forming process where the baby comes out deformed or brain damaged in some way or even with a disease or addiction that might not be detectable at that time. He loves to do this especially if the baby was going to be a significant part of the Earth in some way. The Devil does not do this to all but to many.

With early corruption, the Human has a start in darkness. The Devil will cause malfunctions to a baby to spite the parents or family because he could not corrupt them. There is nothing the Devil won't do or say to spread evil, harm, pain, and suffering to all.

The Devil cannot be trusted and will lie to get anything he wants. And when a Human is too strong with their faith in God, he will send his Demons to them and/or Dark Energies/Entities to tempt, torment, and torture until the Human falls victim to them. However, not all will fall victim. In that case, the Devil will call back the Demons and/or Dark Energies/Entities and try at another time if he feels they are worth it.

The Devil sends Demons throughout the world. He spreads them all over the Earth for the sole purpose of corruption, harm, pain, suffering, and death to Humans and other life forms. They might be sent in the form of other Humans. And even Humans who become trusted friends with each other.

Demons can be a family member, a neighbor, a work associate, a doctor, lawyer, religious leader, a politician, scientist, a teacher, coach, anyone. Every Human is a candidate for corruption by the darkness.

Demons are physical forms that are evil with no regard for Human life nor do they care about the welfare of Humans or any other life form. Their sole purpose is to carry out the orders given by the Devil whom they serve and serve alone.

Demons can come and go. That means if they complete their tasks, they may be dispatched by the Devil to go elsewhere for another task. A Demon can die with the physical form they have if the Devil so desires. The Devil controls everything with the Demons.

A Demon can be assigned to a particular Human to destroy their life or just wreak havoc in it. For example, they may be sent in disguise as a romantic interest to infiltrate the Human's life and when they get in, they start to disrupt the Human's life to try to destroy it and them. If a Human is rich and/or famous, the Demon may have been dispatched by the Devil to ruin them in all ways as to tear down their image, have them make wrong decisions so that they lose money or look bad in the public eye. They may steer them to taking work that is not right or correct for them which could send their career off track or even down the tubes. They will use the Human for money and fame for themselves and try to take the spotlight. There is nothing this Demon will not do because this is their task from the Devil.

However, if a particular Human is very enticing, or the Human might not be fooled by a Demon for some reason, the Devil my do his own dirty work and disguise himself as that Human's romantic partner, business partner, or trusted friend.

If the Demon is successful in destroying the Human's life, then after their task is complete, they will move on to someone else. The Demon can even be tasked to stay with the Human until their body passes from the Earthly plane. And this Demon will drain the energy and life force slowly from the Human.

If the Human has a vice or addiction, then the Demon will encourage the Human to continue and do more of it. If the Human smokes and wants to quit or not, the Demon might cause the Human to be around people that smoke or take a part in a movie where the character smokes. This makes it hard for the Human to quit, and it adds to the destruction of their health. If the Human drinks alcohol, the Demon will encourage them to drink more until they become alcohol dependent. They may even encourage the Human to get into an alcohol business. They will push anything that is bad and negative on the Human or encourage the Human to continue with their vice until it causes illness or death to them.

That's just some examples which is bad enough. But Demons work on the minds of people as well. They either encourage them to do wrong things or subject the Human to bad and try to force them to do things they don't want to or is not right for them.

Demons will also try to physically harm a Human if they need to and even try to have a Human harm or kill another Human. If they were dispatched to destroy a Human's life, they will stop at nothing. They will also steer the Human away from loved ones in order to isolate them so that they can manipulate and work their darkness on the Human. They will start lies and trouble between the Human and their loved ones and/or friends and even business associates. The Demon's sole purpose is to destroy if that was their task from the Devil.

There are Demons that have been tasked just to cause heartache and pain to Humans. They will enter a Human's life, learn all about it, and then use what they need to cause that heartache and pain whether they use them physically, or disrupt their emotional, or mental state.

Demons can be so convincing that the Human fully trusts them and even think they are friends. They may also completely trust the Demon to the point of allowing them full access to their life and personal information. Demons are cunning like the Devil.

There are other types of Demons who terrorize Humans and anyone associated with them. Their sole purpose is to cause complete fear. The fear can escalate to a problematic state for the Human whereas they need to see a doctor or doctors. They can cause a Human to feel that they are going insane. They can cause a Human to have depression and to a severe level where the Human starts medication or ends up in a mental facility. And the Demons laugh and love this. The worse the Human gets the more they love it.

Even medications a Human may take cannot stop a Demon. A Demon can drive a Human to take their own life. This happens to so many Humans. It is common to hear that a Human who has taken their life have another Human say about them that they had many Demons that they could no longer fight. However, their definition of Demons as they meant it was that the Human had depression, did drugs, or couldn't get over the passing of a loved one, a failed romantic relationship or marriage, etc. But the reality is not exactly that. It is an actual evil Demon that drove the Human to take their own life.

Dark Energies/Entities can do this as well. However, the difference is that they are not physical beings like Demons are. They can take a form but not stay in that form. But they can enter into a Human or other life form and cause them to think and do terrible things to themselves and others.

The Devil is also in charge of Dark Energies/Entities. They also serve the Devil and the Devil alone. Dark

Energies/Entities also roam the Earthly plane, other Planets, Galaxies, and Dimensions. And they reside in the in-between realm where all Spirits roam. Dark Energies/Entities attach themselves to Humans and other life forms that Astral Travel, meditate, play music, and even in their dreams and come to the Earthly plane to wreak havoc and/or do harm. They even enter the Earthly plane through portals.

Once a Dark Energy/Entity enters the Earthly plane they can go anywhere. They even travel to other Planets, Galaxies, and Dimensions. They love roaming the Earthly plane spreading darkness, fear, harm, corruption, etc.

A Human might not even know that a Dark Energy/Entity had attached themselves to them. A Dark Energy/Entity could attach themselves to the Human in an awake state as they go about their everyday business. They can be out and about having fun, or running errands, at work, and come home with a Dark Energy/Entity attached to them and release them into their home.

They will eventually know that there is something evil or sinister around them because the Dark Energy/Entity will start to cause problems for them in some way. They may just move things around the house, break things, open doors and windows, spill things, and the like. Or they will start to terrorize the Human deeper in their life. They may physically touch the Human or shove them or cause them not to be able to sleep at night. They will appear in the Human's bedroom or any room and terrorize them. And yes, they can touch a Human. A Human can feel them.

If the Dark Energy/Entity has entered through a portal, it might be inside a Human's home somewhere. That portal would need to be found and closed. Just using sage to clear a home will not banish a Dark Energy/Entity. A Spiritual or Metaphysical specialist may be needed to help with this.

If the Dark Energy/Entity entered the home with the Human, a full cleansing of the home will be necessary and still a professional might be needed. If a portal is closed in the home, a full cleansing and blessing will also be needed and the portal sealed otherwise the Dark Energy/Entity can return.

Certain musical or sound frequencies can open portals. So, if a Human plays or listens to meditation or Spiritual music, or any music for that matter that might emit a certain frequency, that might open a portal unbeknownst to the Human until they start to experience the Dark Energy/Entity or have negative feelings. Then a professional would have to be brought in to find the portal and close it. And even after clearing out the space doesn't mean the darkness won't come back. But it may offer relief for a while.

Dark Energies/Entities do not hang around a home all day long. They actually roam around and come back to terrorize and torture the Human. And they mostly like to terrorize at night.

Dark Energies/Entities can enter Human physical bodies. They can enter while the baby is forming in the womb, or at any given time in the Human's life.

The Devil will dispatch Dark Energies/Entities to either terrorize the Human from the outside or inside of the Human's body. If on the outside, they will do things in the surrounding area of the Human to tease, frustrate, and make the Human angry. If they terrorize from the inside of a Human's physical body, they can cause the Human to do things that are out of the norm for that Human. It could be things that scale from harmless but annoying to serious and harmful.

Dark Energies/Entities can cause a Human to change their thinking from normal to abnormal. They can cause a Human to become violent even if they were never violent before. Dark Energies/Entities can cause emotional and mental disorders to the point of harming themselves and/or others. And even to the point of taking the life of another Human or life form. Many times, a Human can do something terrible and not remember it if possessed by a Dark Energy/Entity.

When Dark Energies/Entities take over a Human it is called possession. Dark Energies/Entities can be exorcised out of a Human by a professional but not always. Dark Energies/Entities will leave a Human body when they want to, are ready to, or instructed to by the Devil. They will leave a Human body if the Human's physical body no longer ceases to exist. At that point the Devil will dispatch them somewhere else or they will return to the in-between realm, or even just roam around the Earthly plane wreaking havoc on others and possessing other Humans.

Humans can be possessed by Dark Energies/Entities at any age or time in their lives. When the Dark Energies/Entities are told to strike, then that's when they strike. Dark Energies/Entities have caused many Humans to have emotional and mental issues and breakdowns. Some never to recover and that is because the Dark Energy/Entity is within them.

Many people do not believe in Dark Energies/Entities. They do not believe in possession. They do not believe there is a Devil or Demons either. But they do exist. And they do wreak havoc wherever they go. Their mission is solely to cause evil to all Humans and other life forms. And they aren't going to stop any time soon or ever.

The Devil, Demons, and Dark Energies/Entities hate all Humans and life forms that are good and of the light. They hate God, so if a Human or other life form serves God, they will try to corrupt the Human and other life forms. If they cannot corrupt them, they will then torment, torture, and even harm or kill them.

Darkness hates the light. Darkness hates all that is good. Darkness hates all Humans who love and serve God.

Humans and other life forms will always be part of **the battle between "good" and "evil."**

Chapter 12

Conflict Amongst Darkness

Demons and Dark Energies/Entities don't always get along. Although both are under and serve the Devil, there is conflict between them.

Demons will fight with other Demons for position and rank. And they will fight each other for the spotlight with the Devil. As Humans compete in sports and in their workplace for promotion, Demons compete as well except it is to be placed higher with the Devil. They fight to rank higher than each other. They want the spotlight and promotion from the Devil to get to do the evilest jobs.

Demons will fight with Dark Energies/Entities for the same thing. Dark Energies/Entities are of a lesser rank than Demons as they have other assignments than Demons. Dark Energies/Entities will defend themselves against Demons but they would rather not bother because they are not ranked as Demons are. Dark Energies/Entities are freer spirited but in a negative way. Demons just love to fight and be evil.

Demons rank quite high on the scale near the Devil. And if they get too pushy the Devil will make sure that they get shoved down the rank. The Devil is still the most powerful darkness in the Universe. And no matter how hard a Demon may try, they can never overtake the Devil. It is the same with

Dark Energies/Entities. But that still does not stop them from trying because they are evil through and through.

Demons try to work behind the Devil's back but as God sees all, so does the Devil. And just because the Demons cannot fool the Devil, it doesn't stop them from trying. Demons aren't in constant competition with each other but from time to time they are. And they can become quite evil to each other. If things get out of hand, the Devil will step in and restore things to their normal. There is also punishment for them as well. Yes, even Demons get punished. They may get an assignment taken away from them or not be assigned a task for a period of time or not get a task they wanted.

The dark Spirit world is similar to Humans living their lives on the Earthly plane in that the Demons get punished, get tasks assigned to them, do the job they were tasked, etc. only theirs is all for the torment, torture, and possible death of Humans and other life forms.

Dark Energies/Entities come and go more freely spreading their darkness, possessing living beings, and causing torment and much worse. They are not interested in rank. Demons are like military soldiers for the Devil whereas Dark Energies/Entities are freer Spirited. Their energies are lighter than Demons but can be just as deadly. However, they prefer to stay out of the Demons way and do their own thing and carry out the orders of the Devil.

Demons will not stop conflict with each other because they love to fight. They love to cause harm even to each other. They love to step over one another for a higher ranking. And they will still at times try to overthrow the Devil. If a Demon tries more than once to overthrow the Devil, the Devil may destroy that Demon. And the Devil does that to keep them in line, and cause the Demons to fear him.

Humans on the earthly plane will experience what the Demons do with each other because the Demons will cause that to happen to the Humans. The Demon will be behind the Human's negative or evil actions. So, when a Demon is reprimanded so to speak, he will punish a Human purposely to act out his anger.

Darkness will always have conflict with each other. They themselves will battle within their own evil darkness.

Chapter 13

Protection Against the Darkness

When you suspect demonic energy is at work; or negativity, or a feeling of heaviness is weighing you down; or things feel confusing, chaotic and toxic; or you are stuck in a pattern or habit that you know is not good for you, there are things that you can do. For example, recognize that you are most likely being plagued by the Devil, Demons or Dark Energies/Entities.

To try to get them out of your thoughts if you have negative or worse thoughts, you can use words to tell them that you know it is them and not coming from you. Tell them that you know what is happening and refuse to accept it. This takes great faith and belief and needed to be said with conviction otherwise the darkness will not comply. Doing this is used as a deterrent.

Prayer is another way to try to ward off demonic activity. Stay strong in God. Stay strong in your religious beliefs and close the doors if you suspect demonic energy is at play in your life.

Although meditation can be a way of attracting the darkness, it is another way of repelling them as well, as it connects you with a higher power providing protection.

If the demonic energy is too strong and nothing else is working, continue with your belief and prayers, but exorcism may be necessary to remove demonic entities from a person or place. Exorcism is the extreme when nothing else is working to remove the demonic activity from a Human or even a place. However, this must be done by a professional, most commonly, a religious figure. Exorcism should never be taken lightly or done by a Human who is unsure how to do it or is a novice otherwise, it could worsen the demonic activity.

Humans and other life forms have to realize that the Devil, Demons, and Dark Energies/Entities hate God, and hate all who love and worship him. So, protection is the key.

Humans can call on the Archangels and Angels to help protect them and/or fight the battle. The more protection the Human has the less likely the darkness can enter their physical body, mind, their home, and any other location.

Humans and other life forms need not spend their lives walking around in fear; however, it is necessary to be mindful of their lives and how they live them. They need to be mindful of whom they associate with, whom they become friends with, whom they work with, etc. Humans need not fear each other but just understand that there is darkness that lurks everywhere and to exercise good judgement when going places and dealing with other Humans.

Steering away from Humans who are into darkness or suspected of darkness is imperative. Those Humans have been infected and/or corrupted and they want to infect and corrupt other Humans. Staying away is a good protective measure. Also, if a Human becomes friendly with another Human that seems harmless and nice and then finds that there is something not right or off with them, steering away from them or removing those Humans from their life is necessary.

Humans should stay away from joining dark religious groups or cults. They should stay away from Humans that worship darkness or the Devil. That could lead the Human down a dark path that they might not recover from. So, the best protection would be to stay clear of those dark Humans.

Avoidance of the darkness in all forms is a great protection measure.

When a Human leaves their home each time, they should visualize a white protective light surrounding their entire physical body and deem this as their protection while out and about in the world. White light is a great protection tool against the darkness. Even though darkness hates Humans of the light, this is different in that they hate the outward shining light therefore avoiding it. This means that a Human can go out and about their daily life with a shield of protected white light. Although there are some powerful darknesses out there, this helps and is a great deterrent.

Carrying protection crystals and stones is another way of protecting a Human against the darkness while inside their dwelling or while out and about in the world. These crystals and stones can be held in the hand, put in a pocket, carried in a purse, worn in jewelry form, and more. See **Chapter 20** for the list of the crystals, stones, and their protection properties.

But above all, God is a Human's and other life form's greatest protection.

Humans and other life forms are always going to **battle between "good" and "evil,"** so protection in all forms will always be necessary while they live their lives on the Earthly plane, on other Planets, and in other Galaxies, and Dimensions.

Chapter 14

Science versus Spirit

Science seems to always have a "scientific" explanation to a Spiritual happening, situation, or experience.

They love to blame seeing Spirits or other than Human life forms as a problem or temporary problem with the Human's brain or eyesight.

When a Human is on their death bed getting ready for the physical body to die and their Soul to pass, the Human may very well see passed over loved ones, including pets, or religious figures, even Jesus or God in the room with them waiting for their body to die so that they can be escorted to the afterlife with no fear for the dying Human.

In Science, they will explain this away with the brain is dying and causing hallucinations. One part of that is true. The brain is definitely dying, but the false part is that the dying Human is not having hallucinations. They truly are seeing Spirit and/or their passed over loved ones.

When a Human that is not dying sees Spirits or passed over loved ones, Science loves to say that the Human may have had trauma to their head causing this to happen. If the Human is taking medication(s), Science will say it's from the medication(s) that is being taken by that Human. Although, some medication(s) can mess with the mind as can trauma to the brain, it is not necessarily the cause for the Human seeing Spirits or passed over loved ones.

If a Human seeing Spirits and/or passed over loved ones is not taking medication(s), Science may suggest that that Human visit their medical doctor and have various tests performed. They may even suggest that the Human also see an ophthalmologist to have their eyes tested as well.

If a Human drinks alcohol or is an alcoholic, Science will blame seeing Spirits and/or passed over loved ones on the Human being inebriated. They will say that the brain/mind is affected by the alcohol causing the Human to see things that aren't there, or imagining things or someone is there when they are not.

A Human can then go through test after test with the end result being that nothing is wrong with them. Science can convince some Humans that something is definitely wrong and that they should go for more tests. Science can be the one causing an issue for a Human that has no issue at all. They really may be seeing Spirits and/or their passed over loved ones.

And Humans are not the only living beings on Earth, on other Planets, in other Galaxies, and Dimensions. So, for Science to believe or say another life form does not exist, therefore is not seen by a Human, or that the Human is seeing things that are not there is ludicrous. Alien life forms roam the Earthly plane as do Spirits and passed over loved ones. Per God, that is a fact.

Spirits and passed over loved ones can show themselves at any time to a Human who is still alive on the Earthly plane whether the Human is on medication(s) or not.

Spirits and passed over loved ones are known for entering a Human's dreams. Depending on the dream, this is called a visitation. Of course, Science has their explanation for this as well. Science says the Human has too much on their mind and is releasing in their dreams. Or, they are going through emotional times and they are processing in their dreams. Depending on the dream, not always the case. Spirit and/or passed over loved ones definitely visit Humans in their dreams because this is the time when Humans are at rest and their mind isn't dealing with the activities of the day. When the Human is relaxed sleeping, it is easier for Spirit and/or loved ones to be able to contact the Human to give a message or messages and for the Human to actually remember at times when they wake up.

Science also does not believe in a Human seeing or experiencing the Devil, Demons, and/or Dark Energies/Entities. According to Science, Humans plagued by any of the darkness must have physical, emotional, and/or mental issues due to medication, addiction, or brain trauma or malfunction, or some other scientific explanation. There is always a perfectly good "scientific" explanation to them. They are so far off the mark with all of that. This darkness exists whether they believe it or not. There is no scientific reasoning that can explain this. It is real, and it happens and exists daily.

Science always feels that there is a logical explanation to something or a happening, and that their explanations are true and correct. Just not so. Not in the case of Spirit.

Science also does not believe in Psychics or Mediums. Psychics are Humans that have the ability to see, feel, know, and hear beyond the Earthly veil.

Mediums are Humans that can communicate with the passed over and even with other life forms on Earth, on other Planets, in other Galaxies, and Dimensions. Science would put Psychics and Mediums in the category of having mental or emotional issues, or a problem with their brain or any other part of their body that would cause them to believe that they can communicate with or see other beings alive or dead.

Science has their beliefs and Spiritual Humans have theirs. This is where Science can also battle with religious groups. It has been done in the past, is done now, and most likely always will be a battle between the two. Science and religion will always have a problem with each other over Science versus Spirit.

In this case Spirit is considered "good" and Science is considered "evil." Although Science is not completely wrong in some of their findings or necessarily bad, however in the case of Spirits and passed over loved ones being seen and/or heard by Humans whether when they are awake or in their dreams, and Humans able to connect with the afterlife and other places in the Universe is considered **the battle between "good" and "evil."**

Chapter 15

Medical versus Holistic

"Medical" means the science or practice of medicine to the treatment of illness and injuries. Medical can be related to the diagnosis, treatment, and prevention of diseases and injuries.

"Holistic" means considering something as a whole, rather than just its individual parts. There is emphasis on the interconnectedness and interdependence of all aspects. It emphasizes the well-being of the whole Human which includes the physical, mental, emotional, social, and Spiritual aspects of health.

I'm sure you are wondering how this fits into **the battle between "good" and "evil."** It very much fits into that.

Let me preface what I am about to write about doctors and medicine with there is a need for surgeons, doctors, and medicine for Humans and all life forms. In a life-or-death situation, doctors and medicine are very welcomed. Their scientific minds and the medicines used for a life and death situation is needed in this day and age and for a very long time beforehand.

Most doctors, if not pretty much all, from the beginning of doctors and medicine have treated symptoms of the patient. They diagnosed the best they could when given the symptoms of the patient and handed out medicine to treat that symptom or those symptoms. If that didn't work further study was done and then further medicine was given.

As the years and decades passed doctors became more educated and exposed to the new illnesses and diseases that arose with Humans. Medical machines were invented to help in the diagnosis of an illness or disease. Bloodwork was performed and through the study and evaluation a possible illness was diagnosed and then medicine was disbursed to that Human to try to help with the pain or whatever illness they had.

There was a lot of trial and error and still is to this day because of all the new viruses and diseases that pop up on the Earthly plane. More and more studies had to be done and was done. And more and more medicine was prescribed to the patient to treat and maybe cure what they had. But not all had illnesses that could be cured, so their illnesses were treated with medicine and managed until the Human's life on the Earthly plane ceased to exist or they eventually died from their illness.

For decades and maybe centuries medicine was given by doctors to treat a symptom but not the root of the problem. They handed over medicine as the treatment and/or cure. But not all were cured.

Side effects from the medicines were felt by many throughout the years and decades, and maybe even centuries which ended up being a whole other problem added to the illness they already had. Some felt side effects so strongly that it overshadowed the illness they were dealing with initially. So, they were told to either continue to see if they got used to the medicine whereas the side effects would stop, or they were told to stop the medicine and was given another medicine to take its place to see if that helped. Or they were given an additional medicine to take with the original one so as to combat the side effects of the original medicine.

Still the patient was not healing or was healed from their illness because their symptoms were being treated instead of getting to the root of the illness. What was causing the illness in the first place? Lots of guesses and at times doctors would even say they were stumped and then give another medicine for the patient to try in hopes that that medicine did the trick in stopping the side effects of the first medicine and cure the illness. Just a complete mess.

This happens on a daily basis. More and more medicines are prescribed for the Human's illness symptoms instead of getting to the root of the illness.

If an illness such as a problem with a treatable organ illness was diagnosed, then the medicine given may have helped or did help with that organ in bringing it back to functioning properly. Not always the case however.

There have been too many to count missed diagnoses and wrong diagnoses. Of course, medicine was prescribed to the Human patient and it either caused the illness to worsen or at worst case scenario, the patient died.

For so many patients, medicine is freely prescribed over and over again. Freely given to Humans that cannot sleep at night. Medicine freely given to Humans if their emotions felt low. Medicine given freely if the Human wanted to lose weight without changing to a healthy diet with exercise. And medicines freely given to Humans who could not lose weight no matter how healthy they ate or how much they exercised. My point is that medicines are dispensed too freely for the littlest thing.

Maybe a Human cannot get clear skin so they run to the doctor and the doctor prescribes internal and/or external medicine without even asking about what kinds of foods that that Human eats or what they drink or does not drink. Never asking if they have stresses in their life adding to the problem. There is no getting to the root of the problem, only treating the symptoms. An excuse from the doctor might be, well the Human is at an adolescent age and that age is normal to have poor skin so it is okay to prescribe medicine for them.

Now, not to put all the blame on doctors as there are plenty of Humans who want medicine for anything and everything. But the blame would definitely go on the doctor who caves in and just hands over the medicine without trying to get to the root of the Human's illness whether emotional, mental, and/or physical.

And medicine is prescribed for the least little problem a Human is having. Many problems can be solved or even cured if the doctor took the time to really research and work with the patients. There is a lot of here take this and you'll feel better soon. And let me know if it doesn't work and we'll try something else.

And not all medicines prescribed to Humans are prescriptions written from a doctor, but prescribed to the patient by the doctor to take some over the counter medicine. And that surely is no cure for their illness. It is only a band aid or temporary fix called treating the symptom.

Cancer is no joke. It can attack any Human at any time in their life. But there are always doctors and medical facilities wanting donations from Humans to help find a cure. There is no cure really. There are so many different forms of cancer and strikes any part of the Human body inside and/or outside.

Cancer medicine may be disbursed to the Human. Chemotherapy and radiation therapy may be prescribed for the Human depending on the type of cancer, where in or out of the body it is, and what organ or organs it has affected and how far it has possibly spread within the Human body. Many Humans who have cancer are able to live longer lives due to some medicines given to them, or the type of treatment they receive.

Some Humans die slower and some faster depending on their type of cancer and the progression it has taken. Some Humans beat cancer by the medicine or treatment they receive, or by surgery if that is warranted. And other Humans can have years added to their lives by taking some cancer medicines and/or treatments but most will eventually pass from it. And the fortunate Humans that beat cancer, are still faced with the fear or fact that it can return at any point, however they pray it doesn't.

But there is no real cure for cancer. The majority of doctors, big drug companies, and even some of the governments don't want the cure. If there was a cure there would be too many people on Earth. If there was a cure, the doctors might look good in their profession but on the other hand they make tons of money prescribing medicine, and the drug companies make billions. They all work together. Sickening actually.

Most doctors do not take the time to understand that it isn't just the physical body that needs healing from the illness but the emotional, mental, and even Spiritual parts of the Human need to be treated as well. They all work together to bring total healing to the Human.

By treating the physical body alone for an illness, it can and often does throw off the emotional, mental, and Spiritual in a

Human. A physical illness can be so devastating to a Human whether the illness is slight or severe, that it causes them stress and heartache affecting their emotions and making their physical illness possibly worse. It can affect their mental status throwing them into a mental illness even wanting to harm or kill themselves due to the fear and nature of their illness, and maybe feeling like there is no cure for them and that they will die.

And they also need treatment Spiritually because they need to believe in their faith that they can get well, and for them to pray or visit their religion or religious place if they have one for comfort. Or just pray to God or the Angels or whomever they believe in. This can actually give them emotional and mental comfort from the stress of their illness and in turn that helps with the physical healing process. It all goes together, but you will find that most doctors don't go that far. They will stick with prescribing for the physical body only and treat its symptom.

Doctors have branched off into opening practices where they do believe that the physical, emotional, mental, and Spiritual all must be treated collectively in order to get well. These doctors call themselves Holistic doctors or Holistic practitioners in Holistic Healthcare.

Holistic healthcare focuses on treating the whole Human, which encompasses physical, emotional, mental, and Spiritual well-being, rather than just individual symptoms. It emphasizes the interconnectedness of all aspects of a Human's health. And seeks to address the root causes of the illness. This approach incorporates various methods, including traditional medical treatments, alternative therapies, and lifestyle modifications to promote overall wellness.

The Holistic practitioner assesses a Human's overall health. They not only take into consideration the Human's symptoms but their habits, lifestyle, emotional state, and Spiritual beliefs. This Holistic assessment helps identify potential underlying causes or contributing factors to a Human's health issues. These practitioners aim to address the root causes of illness, rather than just treating the symptoms.

Holistic practitioners often collaborate with other healthcare professionals, such as doctors, therapists, and counselors, to provide a comprehensive and integrated approach to the care. This collaboration ensures that Humans receive the support and resources they need to achieve their health goals. This may involve exploring factors like an unhealthy diet, stress, lack of sleep, or even negative relationships that may be contributing to a Human's health issues.

Holistic healthcare aims at not only physical health but also mental, emotional, and spiritual well-being. This may involve practices like yoga, meditation, art therapy classes, or Spiritual practices.

They encourage the Human to take part in their own healthcare and well-being. This way they have the knowledge and tools to make informed decisions and choices about their lifestyle and health.

Holistic healthcare offers numerous benefits, including improved quality of life, reduced stress and anxiety, enhanced mental and emotional well-being, and a greater sense of purpose and meaning.

It can also help Humans develop healthy coping mechanisms for dealing with life's challenges.

So, depending on a Human's views and beliefs about their own health and how they receive treatment and by whom can definitely be **the battle between "good" and "evil."**

Chapter 16

Human versus Human

In my book **INTERVIEWING GOD**, we talk about Humans and their creation, so, I will not get into that part, although this book touches on that a bit. But I will say that Humans were not created to have conflict with one another. They were created with love and peace to be loving and compassionate towards one another. However, throughout time and with the help of the dark side that changed with many Humans.

The Devil and his crew caused much chaos throughout time for Humans that they became fearful and mistrusting of each other. Not all, but many. As the centuries and decades flew by Humans learned to devise ways to separate themselves from certain Humans. The wealthy Humans started associating with other wealthy Humans. The financially middle-class could associate with the wealthy, their own class and even lower-class. The financially lower-class Humans could associate with middle-class Humans but not many with the wealthy nor did many wealthy want to associate with the lower-middle class. Then there were the Humans who were considered poor barely getting by financially, and then the destitute Humans. Those, most of the wealthy Humans wanted nothing to do with.

The classes have changed throughout the decades due to the economy and the fluctuation of the Humans' income. With time there became the wealthy, middle-class, and poor with poor including the destitute Humans. And in today's society that gap is rapidly closing to wealthy and poor cutting out much of the middle-class and completely cutting out lower middle-class. The middle-class Humans are now struggling almost as much as the poor. Quite frightening.

Some of the disassociation between the wealthy and lower classes was due to the lower classes not having the money to participate or keep up with what the wealthy were able to afford to do. Other disassociation reasons were that many of the wealthy Humans looked down on the lower-class Humans. They felt that they were better due to having a lot of money. Some had the King and Kingdom complex.

The wealthy could afford to have other Humans work for them in their businesses and in their homes as servants in some fashion. Most of the lower classes could not afford that and usually worked for the wealthy.

As life progressed, there became some unrest with the classes. The lower classes wanted what the upper-class wealthy had. So, they either took the route of working hard to get there or to join the dark forces of jealousy and steal or cheat their way to a higher financial status. This caused a lot of unrest and eventual battle between Human and Human.

In today's society, Humans battle each other for wealth, for positions in a business, for positions in government, for promotions at work, and much more.

Humans battle each other to keep their wealth and possessions from being stolen by other Humans. Others battle each other to try to gain power, status, and even fame. Battles can get quite ugly and dangerous.

Humans had to hire security to keep their property and businesses safe from other Humans. The wider the financial gap became in the classes the more problems arose with Human against Human.

For the very poor and destitute Humans, the battle was mostly for survival. They needed food, water, shelter, clothing, and much more. Unable to provide that for themselves for one reason or another, they battled with other Humans for those items whether it be with other poor Humans or Humans who had a lot more than them.

Money, power, and status caused many Humans to become corrupted. One Human fighting another Human for more money, more power, more status. Some Humans felt the more of that they had the more they could get and the more Humans they could control. A very vicious circle. They stepped into the darkness of greed.

Humans not only battle each other for material goods but for land and the takeover of countries. Winning those battles gives great power, money, and status.

Humans even battle each other in sports. There is what is called competition. Each Human wants to win in their sport. And with each win comes more money, more power, and more status.

There are competitions not only in sports but in other arenas such as baking competitions, dog show competitions, motorcycle competitions, car racing competitions, food eating competitions, marathons, bicycling competitions, beauty pageants, and so much more. And in some of these competitions, the darkness has entered in and officials are paid a lot of money to make sure a certain Human wins their competition. And in other cases, an actual competitor is paid money to throw the competition and allow a certain other to win. And in darker cases, no money but threats of harm or death if a particular Human isn't allowed to win.

Humans are constantly battling each other and the darkness as well on a daily basis. It has become the norm. And every Human wants to have more than they have. Humans have become greedy, and what they have is never enough. Not all Humans feel this way but most. And the more some Humans have the more they want and can never be satisfied with what they have or achieved.

There are many Humans that have a need to keep up with the Joneses. That means that they do not have the financial capacity to do what someone or some others do or have what others have. But they will even go into debt to try to keep up those appearances. It is a form of sickness which definitely comes from the darkness. This trying to keep up becomes a battle for them. Their battle may spread and affect their family members or friends in a negative way. And the more negatively it affects the Humans the more the darkness loves it. And the darkness will try to keep that negativity going.

The battle between Human and Human has escalated to a high degree due to trying to survive on this planet. And then you have the darkness pushing and shoving Humans deeper into the darkness trying to keep Humans in a fragile state so that there will be more battles between them.

The darkness loves when Humans fight, argue, get in over their heads financially, steal from other Humans, struggle, and so much more. The more Humans battle each other, the more the darkness loves it and pushes harder. Darkness loves the greedy Humans because the darkness is able to infect those Humans deeper.

They love the Humans who cause trouble for other Humans. They love the Humans who cheat other Humans. They love when Humans steal from other Humans. They love when Humans fight with other Humans. And Humans, not all, but many accommodate the darkness by all their negative, to put it lightly, actions towards each other.

Now, there are the good and law-abiding Humans who have to deal with the dark infected Humans. It is not easy to deal with the dark Humans. That in and of itself is a feat. It takes a strong willed and faith in God Human to do so. For them, it could be a daily battle. And the temptations of the darkness and dark Humans is constant. Each Human would love to have nice and wonderful things in life. Each Human would love to not worry about their finances. Each Human would love to win competitions. Each Human would love to be happy and stress free. But life on this planet does not always allow that for all Humans.

Humans need to learn to be happy with what they do have. God gave all Humans free will to do anything they want or be anything they want in their lifetime on the Earthly plane. Most Humans have choices to do good things for themselves and others. There are some Humans that may be born into an unfortunate situation but at some point, they have a choice to take the path of light and God or to take the path of darkness and the Devil. All Humans are faced with that at some point in their lives. And the darkness will try the hardest to corrupt and draw the Humans to the dark side. Hopefully, the Humans chooses the path of light and God.

For Humans, there will always be **the battle between "good" and "evil."**

Chapter 17

Human versus Animal

Humans and *Animals* were created to work and live in harmony with each other. That includes all life forms on Earth.

The evolvement of Humans and animals changed that throughout time. Because of the scarcity of plant food in different parts of Earth, Humans turned to animals and other life forms as a source of food. Humans were not created to eat anything other than plant foods.

The eating of other life forms changed the physical, emotional, and mental structure of Humans. Humans became more aggressive throughout time by eating animal meat. Humans that ate other life forms other than meat or meat like life forms developed a lesser degree of aggressiveness, however, nevertheless still aggressive but to a lesser degree that's all.

The Human body developed differently than it was created to do. The love emotion towards each other, animals, and other life forms grew lesser. To kill another life form became somewhat emotionless and to other Humans it was completely emotionless. They could kill and eat the animal or other life form without remorse.

Soon many Humans became hunters of the animals for their source of food and then for sport as the Humans grew in intelligence. They also used the murdered animal or other life form for their furs, skins, and bones. They used that as clothing, bedding, weapons, parts of housing/shelter, and more.

Since animals started being hunted as food, they themselves grew in fear and some in aggression as a defense. That lead to some animals evolving into automatic aggressors towards Humans.

Also, animals and other life forms were not created to kill one another for any reason. But the same as Humans in some parts of the Earth, they could not find food and animals started killing other animals and life forms as a source of food in order to survive. And some grew extremely aggressive in killing Humans for defense and/or food.

But it was because of Humans that the aggression of animals began. It became a battle between Humans, animals, and other life forms.

To this day, there is little to no regard Humans have for animals and other life forms. They kill at will. If a Human feels an animal or other life form is a bother to them, they want them gone in whatever way they can make that happen. For most Humans, life of an animal or other life form has little to no meaning or value. There is little to no regard for life. Some Humans have little to no regard for the lives of other Humans.

Now, what started all this aggression towards animals and other life forms was not just for survival. Oh no. We can take a look at the dark side for that.

Yes, the Devil had a hand in all of it. Tempting Humans to kill even when not necessary as in needing food to survive. He sent his Demon henchmen throughout Earth spreading their dark disease upon Humans, animals, and other life forms. Dark Energies/Entities entered into Humans, animals, and other life forms corrupting them. This did not happen to all Humans, animals, and other life forms, but it surely did to many and that disease spread like the plague.

The Devil pushed for Humans to kill animals and other life forms as sport. Kill for no good reason was enjoyment for the Devil, Demons, and Dark Energies/Entities.

The Dark Energies/Entities loved to get into the minds of Humans and corrupt until the Human went along with it. Their minds were tormented and tortured until they could not stand it any longer. This grew with the evolvement of Humans, animals, and other life forms.

To this day Humans, animals, and other life forms are possessed by the darkness. They are tempted, tormented, and tortured into doing things that are bad.

There is no reason why a Human should have trophies of poor animals with their heads hanging on the wall for the Human to enjoy and boast about. There is no reason why a poor animal was killed so that a Human could have their skin with fur, and at times head attached, laying on their floor as a carpet and trophy. And the Humans who partook and still partake in all of that are of the darkness. If they aren't corrupted by the darkness then they, themselves are Demons.

Humans kill on a daily basis whether they do it on purpose or by accident. When a Human walks down the street, they could accidentally step on insects unbeknownst to them. That is still considered killing a life. However, if they see the insects and step on them anyway then that is on purpose and called murder.

Humans do not want to be bothered by certain animals or other life forms because they fear them, or do not want them near their home or family. There are many reasons Humans have for killing. Some just don't like the look of the animal or other life form so they want them gone or dead. To rid an animal or other life form just because a Human doesn't want it around is considered killing if they cause that animal to die on purpose. Even putting up strips to catch flies or other insects is killing on purpose. To set out traps that have poison in them or snaps and the animal or other life form dies, is killing on purpose. If a Human collects insects for example, and displays dead ones as their collection, that is participating in their death indirectly. There are so many more examples of Humans killing on a daily basis whether on purpose or by accident. If by accident, a Human should ask forgiveness from God.

Humans have become numb to the killing of animals and other life forms accepting it as a part of life. They accept killing of some of those life forms as necessary. They do not care how the animal or other life form dies just as long as they are not bothered by them any longer. And Humans show their children by doing so that it is okay to kill certain life forms with no remorse.

Thankfully, groups of Humans formed throughout time to protect animals and other life forms from the hands of evil Humans. Humans that have been corrupted by the darkness, and Demons posing as Humans.

Unfortunately, the growing darkness continues and there are not enough caring, compassionate Humans to help save and care for animals and other life forms on Earth. Sadly, there is a high percentage of Humans who stay neutral and a high percentage of Humans who are corrupted or possessed by the darkness. And a lower percentage of Humans who help or try to help.

Many Humans have lost regard for life in any form and that includes other Humans. Humans killing on purpose for self-defense, or in order to defend another is one thing. For a Human to kill on purpose for the sake of killing is another and that's called murder.

There is ever **the battle between "good" and "evil."**

Chapter 18

Humans – The Battle Within

The *Human* brain, mind can be described as nothing less than powerful. It has the capability to heal the physical body which some would consider a miracle. It is not a miracle; it was designed by God to do that.

The Human mind can see reality but it can also create fantasy. Many creative Humans tap into this part of their mind. As a Human ages, they can recall memories of their experiences in life even when they are chronologically old. And some Humans can see future events.

But with the good of the mind also comes the not so good. Humans can be plagued by sad or tragic memories of their past. The mind can haunt and torment them with these memories. And the mind can also haunt and torment the Human with thoughts of what the future can or may bring for them.

The Human mind can be a beautiful tool or it can be a death sentence.

Humans not only face battles with other Humans or animals, they have battles within their own minds. There is that internal struggle.

The battle between "good" and "evil" is not always viewed as an external conflict but also as an internal struggle within individuals, where they wrestle with their own desires, temptations, and moral choices.

Humans often battle within themselves about internal conflicts like fears, doubts, and limiting beliefs. This can manifest as struggling to reconcile desires with beliefs, or facing the emotional and psychological challenges of difficult life circumstances.

Humans have internal struggles which often stem from their insecurities, doubts about themselves, and fears of failure or rejection.

Humans also deal with moral dilemmas. They may face situations where their beliefs clash with their actions or the choices they have to make.

Humans battle with ego versus integrity. Sometimes, their ego can push them toward choices that compromise their values.

Social pressure is another battle for Humans. Societal pressures can create internal conflicts as they navigate different expectations and demands.

Ideally, instead of Humans fighting against their inner struggles, they can learn to accept them as part of the Human experience and use them as opportunities for growth.

Ideally, the goal may not necessarily be to eliminate all internal conflicts, but rather to find a balance and create greater harmony within themselves.

We can go on and on about Human internal conflicts, struggles, and battles but with all that has been said, most of what Humans struggle with is not caused by their own minds. And accepting conflicts and struggles doesn't work for many Humans and isn't going to fix a lot of Humans either. It will be the understanding of where most of those thoughts and feelings come from or what has caused them.

The darkness is the culprit and has a great deal to do the struggling mind of a Human. The darkness wants to keep Humans confused, struggling inside and outside, disliking or hating themselves, having internal struggles about what is right and what is wrong, and so much more.

The darkness does not want Humans to have balance and harmony within their lives. Darkness wants Humans to have societal pressure and allow it to emotionally and mentally torment and torture them.

Even when Humans mistreat each other, darkness is behind that. Darkness wants Humans to turn to the dark side, otherwise they want to destroy the Human, their lives, and all who mean something dear to the Human in whatever way they can. And that means getting inside a Human's head and mind, and even using other Humans to help with the hurt and pain.

When Humans tease and bully other Humans, no matter what age the bullies are, do you think those Humans aren't corrupted by the dark? They absolutely are. And some very corrupted Humans will bully to the point that the Human being bullied takes their life. Then the darkness is happy.

Believe me, the darkness is quite evil and will not stop as long as there are Humans who can be corrupted and/or possessed.

There is always going to be **the battle between "good" and "evil"** even if it is only within.

Chapter 19

God versus The Devil

There has always been **the battle between "good" and "evil,"** and the struggle or battle between *God* and the *Devil* is and has always been real.

God is of love and compassion and has created that in all life forms. Humans and other life forms were meant to love and live in harmony with each other. This included all life forms on other Planets, in other Galaxies, and Dimensions.

God is the creator of all in the Universe and beyond. Humans and other life forms were created to be peaceful and to spread love and peace throughout Earth, other Planets, Galaxies, and Dimensions. Love and peace were meant to be spread from ancestor to ancestor, from generation to generation, from one lifetime to another lifetime. This was to be from the beginning of existence through the end of existence.

This was God's will and plan because of his love for all life forms, and because God is love, peace, compassion, harmonious, and beyond the scope of understanding all that is good.

All God asks and has ever asked of Humans and other life forms was to get along with and love each other. He created for Humans a beautiful planet called Earth. One of the most beautiful planets in the Universe.

His plan was for Humans and other life forms to inhabit Earth and multiply themselves and grow the planet. Earth was given everything for Human life forms and other life forms that was needed to sustain and grow life on the planet. God asked of Humans to love and take care of Earth. To keep it free of contaminants in all forms. To continue growing all plant life because that was their form of sustenance. To keep the water clean for other life to continue to grow in and evolve from, and for the consumption of Humans and other life forms. Humans were designed to eat plant life and to drink water. And although not all Humans evolved from the life in the water, all life forms needed and still need water to keep their physical bodies alive.

Earth had everything Humans and other life forms needed. There were the basics with fertile soil, but cultivation was needed to grow more food as Humans and other life forms multiplied. And God was there to call upon for help because he loved all the life forms calling them his children.

The Devil was not a fallen Angel as it has been said and written. The Devil was a Dark Energy/Entity that appeared from a dark part of another Dimension. Dark as in evil. The Devil took on an actual form in this dimension disguised as an Angel. But that could not fool God or any of the other light beings. The Devil was forced out and away from all light beings. The Devil did not corrupt other Angels and draw them to his side.

He headed to Earth because the life that inhabited Earth was of goodness and with love for God. This dark figure now not in Angel form any longer was full of hate. He hated God, all light beings, and all that was good. He had the mission of torment, torture, destruction, and death of anything good. That meant Humans and all other life forms on Earth.

The Devil recruited darkness as in Demons and other Dark Energies/Entities but not as powerful as he. This way the Devil could control and task out his orders to torment, torture, corrupt, destroy, and kill the good life forms on Earth.

The Devil, Demons, and Dark Energies/Entities could travel all over Earth, to other Planets, Galaxies, and Dimensions spreading their evil there as well. But inhabitants on other Planets, in other Galaxies, and Dimensions were not like Humans and other life forms on Earth. Earthly life forms had a light about them, a goodness, a lovingness, compassion, and peace. This was pure fodder for the Devil and his crew. And he and they went to work on the Humans and other life forms trying to corrupt as many as they could and sway to the dark side in whatever form or manner that was successful to do so.

This brought about **the battle between "good" and "evil"** with God and the Devil. The battle never ceases and never will until nothing is left.

Chapter 20

Protection Crystals & Stones

Although there isn't much a Human can do to fully protect themselves from evil other than have strong faith in God, call on the Angels for protection, and strong will to stay on the righteous path, certain Crystals and Stones can offer help of additional protection. Here is a list of them and their Spiritual and Metaphysical properties: Choose the ones best suited for you and your needs. All are amazing.

Amethyst:

A stone well known for protection and stress relief. It is believed to bring clarity and repel negative energy.

Black Obsidian:

This is referred to as the stone of protection for its ability to create a shield against negativity and harmful energies.

Black Tourmaline:

The is the most powerful stone known for its ability to absorb negative energy and to shield and block psychic attacks.

Bloodstone:

Bloodstone provides protection against negative energy, psychic attacks, and emotional vampires. It is said to enhance analytical thinking and facilitate logical decision-making

Clear Quartz:

This is a versatile stone that can be used to repel negative energy, attract positive energy, and balance and regulate overall energy. Put next to or combined with any other crystal and stone, it enhances that crystal's and stone's properties.

Fluorite:

Fluorite is a crystal that houses rainbows. It is highly protective, especially when using on a psychic level. It cleanses and stabilizes the aura, brings clarity of mind, and heightens focus. It helps to bring order to chaos and restore balance.

Hematite:

Hematite is associated with grounding, protection, and emotional stability. It repels negative energy and sends it back to the origin. It also helps balance the body's energy, enhance focus, reduce stress or anxiety, and offers a feeling of security. Hematite also boosts confidence and courage.

Pyrite:

This is a protective and shielding stone that can deflect harm and danger. It is also known to inspire creativity and boost confidence.

Rainbow Tourmaline:

This is excellent for working with chakras and restoring balance to one's energies. This stone promotes joy and happiness by transmuting negative energies and sending them back into the world as unconditional love. It is highly recommended to those seeking emotional support.

Selenite:

This is a purifying stone that can cleanse and create a protective energy shield against negative energies.

Smoky Quartz:

Smoky Quartz is used as an amulet of protection. It helps to dispel negative energy and promotes grounding and stability.

Tiger's Eye:

Tiger's Eye is known for its protective properties. It promotes grounding and stability, helps you stay centered and balanced, especially during challenging times. It boosts courage and confidence, helping you overcome fears and to take action on your goals.

Epilogue

The battle between "good" and "evil" was in the beginning and will be here until the end. The end of Human life, and the end of other life forms on Earth, on other Planets, in other Galaxies, and Dimensions.

But on Earth, Humans are and have been easy to tempt, corrupt, torment, and torture. Not for all but for many. As time went by, the corruption got easier for "evil."

There was no greed in the beginning and soon there was. Greed is a door opener for "evil." And it was due to the "evil" that there was greed. With greed, more and more doors opened to "evil" and therefore more greed.

"Evil" used temptation to open the door of greed. Before money as Humans have known it for a long time, barter of food and goods were used. But even with that, "evil" was able to infiltrate and cause greed. Stealing also began, which was caused by "evil."

Some Humans didn't even realize that stealing and greed was bad because they had nothing or not much to barter with and they themselves and/or their families were hungry, had little to no clothing, little to no shelter, and more. They had to do what they needed to in order to survive. However, being Human, they did feel it wasn't right but had no idea "evil" was behind it. They were encouraged to do wrong, tempted to do wrong. "Evil" entered their minds causing their wrong decisions turning into wrong actions.

Some Humans stuck with stealing, and stealing more and more becoming greedy without bartering something. And soon they were completely corrupted by "evil" and this became their way of life.

Not all Humans stuck with stealing because they knew it was wrong and refused to be tempted. This is because Humans were created with "good" and not "evil."

But with the Humans that didn't care, "evil" had a field day. And corruption of Humans spread and spread. In time, rules and laws were put into place.

There were Kings with large kingdoms. The richer and more powerful they became the greedier they became. Soon there was the very rich and the very poor. The richer they got the more powerful they became. And the more powerful they got the richer they became. "Evil" had conquered Humans. Not all but many.

To this day, it is no different. Greed for power and money run rampant all over Earth. Everyone wants to be rich and everyone wants power. "Evil" loves it. And it is because of "evil' that Earth has these Human inhabitants.

Many Humans will do anything for money. The more money they get the more they want. These Humans have been corrupted by "evil." And these Humans spread that "evil" everywhere. And "evil" loves it and supports them.

Then there are the Humans who still resist temptation and earn their money and status by being on the righteous path and avoiding "evil" as best they can. Life is harder for these Humans but they are "good" and refuse to turn to the dark side just for a buck. These are Humans who put their faith in God and follow God's direction and rules. They are blessed by God for being "good" Humans.

These Humans are tempted by "evil" often because "evil" wants all Humans on the dark side. "Evil" does not want Humans to succeed and do good on their own and follow God. "Evil" hates God and all his followers. "Evil" comes in hard for "good" God loving righteous Humans.

There are doctors, lawyers, politicians, heads of countries, scientists, celebrities, Spiritual leaders, and many prominent and wealthy figures and more who have been somewhat or completely corrupted by "evil."

There is no escaping "evil." It is everywhere a Human goes. The only thing a Human can do is to resist the temptations. If someone steals it is due to "evil." If someone kills it is due to "evil." If someone lies it is due to "evil."

There is **the battle between "good" and "evil"** with each waking day of a Human. Before a Human leaves their home, there is a battle of some sort whether they have viewed something on their television or on their computer or on their cellphone. Heck, there is even a battle with family over getting them out of bed to eat breakfast and off to school. A lesser battle, but nevertheless a battle. And when they leave their home, they are heading into a battle of some sort before their day is done.

A few examples:

Humans battle with homes that need repair whether inside and/or outside. They battle trying to find the best, most reliable, yet affordable company who offers the repair. Then they may have to battle the company they chose if the repair was not properly done or took longer than the quoted repair time, and charged a lot more than the quoted price.

Humans battle in the purchase of a new to them vehicle at a dealer trying to get the vehicle of their choice for an affordable price. And they battle finding the most affordable insurance coverage for that vehicle. And if their vehicle needs repair, they battle over finding a good mechanic and the price the mechanic charges. Hopefully, the mechanic repairs the vehicle properly, otherwise the Human will then battle over the botched repair.

Humans battle in a department store when there is a major sale over merchandise that everyone wants at that very time. And it can get ugly.

Humans battle over who goes first in something. Or if someone cuts in front of them in a line whether standing in a line or in their car in line.

Humans battle over parking spaces.

Humans battle on the road while driving their vehicle. They have to make sure that they get safely from Point A to Point B without incident. And there are times a Human is battling another on the road because of anger over an incident whether done on purpose or by accident. And God forbid there is a vehicle accident as that would be a battle as well.

Humans battle other Humans when there is anger or jealousy over someone or something. Perhaps a Human was up for a promotion at work and another got it instead. Or they were due for a raise and never got it. Or they got the raise and it was not what they expected for all the hard work they put into their job. Or they were expecting a bonus for a job well done or for the holiday and they never received it.

Humans battle over romance. Say a Human is romantically attracted to another and some other Human gets them. This could cause a battle to erupt between them. Or if married and getting divorced, there could be a huge battle especially if children, money, and property are involved.

Humans battle with more serious issues such as illness whether physical, emotional, and/or mental.

The list of battles is quite endless. And behind all the negativity of a battle is the darkness causing disruption and chaos. Darkness and "evil" love when Humans battle. The more severe the battle, the more they love it.

"Evil" loves to divide Humans from one another. They love to cause problems in all forms for Humans from not severe to severe. Even if the battle is temporary, "evil" derives pleasure from that.

"Evil" loves to tempt, and there is always something tempting Humans in some way including to battle over something, to take a wrong path, or to do something that leads them astray from their belief in God and their righteous path.

Always **the battle between "good" and "evil."**

Anything that is not of the light is of the dark

About the Author

Patricia (Patti), is a Celebrity Psychic Medium, Tarot Card Reader, and Author. She was born with her abilities and cultivated them throughout the years incorporating Tarot into her skills.

She reads for celebrities, celebrity families, entertainment producers, directors, etc. She reads for the wealthy and non-wealthy. Most of her clients are referrals. And she continues to receive more and more referrals.

Patricia uses her mediumship abilities to connect her clients to their passed over loved ones receiving validating and healing messages. She uses her psychic ability in her Tarot Card readings giving her clients insight into the past, present, and future. Patricia is also an Empath and able to connect with people on the Earthly plane whom her clients want to know about. She is able to give the client in-depth insight into that person's thoughts and actions. And she delivers messages to her clients with truth and compassion.

Patricia is also a Spiritual Guide. She offers her clients one to one guidance helping them understand what is happening in their lives so that they can gain clarity, begin to heal, and head back to or set on their right path in life.

Another service Patricia offers is Space Clearing & Blessing which is the removal of negative energy that might be lingering in and around the residence, business, or hovering over the land. Negative energies in a home or business can affect the people living and/or working there. After the cleansing, the space is blessed. This Space Clearing & Blessing clears and lightens the energy in the home, business, and on the land bringing with it positive vibrations.

Patricia is an Author and wrote her first book in collaboration with God called **INTERVIEWING GOD**. It is a book of questions posed to God that so many of us have had throughout our lifetime, however, never receiving answers. In this book, God delivered those answers.

This book covers questions about Humans, Aliens, the Devil, Demons, Dark Energies/Entities, the Universe, and God. After reading **INTERVIEWING GOD**, you will come away with answers from God that may leave you surprised and even shocked, however at the very least, you will be enlightened.

This is a must read for Believers, non-Believers, Religious, non-Religious, Spiritual, and non-Spiritual.